HEAVENLY DECEPTION

LIBRARY OF CONGRESS CATALOG CARD NUMBER 80-65291
ISBN 0-8423-1402-4
COPYRIGHT © 1980 BY CHRIS ELKINS
ALL RIGHTS RESERVED
FIRST PRINTING, APRIL 1980
PRINTED IN THE UNITED STATES OF AMERICA

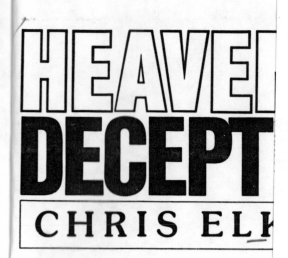

HEAVEN
DECEPT
CHRIS ELK

Tyndale House
Publishers, Inc.
Wheaton, Illinois

This book is dedicated to my parents
MERLE & KAY ELKINS
who, although I misunderstood them at times,
have always loved me.

CONTENTS

PREFACE

There are other books about cults, and probably there will be more. Yet, I would like to think that this book, *Heavenly Deception*, is a special contribution to our understanding of these ever-present "false doctrines" that plague our society. For one thing, this is a story of my involvement with what might be the most powerful and most pervasive cult of our time, the Unification Church. Second, because I am a Christian and have experienced anew God's faithful love, I do not believe that the way to overcome the Unification Church is hate and ostracism, but rather love and concern.

This is a true story, but it is admittedly told from a personal perspective. I do not claim that this is the way the Unification Church operates in every case. It is the way it operated in *my* case. Names have been changed and a few events reconstructed to assure that this could not be construed to be anyone else's story but my own.

There are several people who have been instrumental in putting this book together. First of all, I thank Glenn Igleheart and the Department of Interfaith Witness at the Southern Baptist Home Mission Board for their diligence in helping me share this message across the nation. A particular thanks to Kate Ellen Gruver, whose touch brought healing and perspective into my life. And to the Tyndale House editorial staff, particularly Ken Petersen, whose dedication and perseverance have been admirable.

But to my wife Mini there's a heart-felt expression of appreciation

9

that goes beyond words. Her dreams and constant inspiration are largely responsible for this work. Her strength during long days alone while I have been away speaking or writing can only be credited to her deep and abiding faith in our Savior Jesus Christ. And in him all things have been made possible.

Chris Elkins
18 December 1979

INTRODUCTION

The House Subcommittee on International Organizations
September 27, 1976
Washington, D.C.

They seemed concerned for my safety.

The guard, a strangely quiet and fidgety man, had ushered Greg and me across Constitution Avenue and into the Rayburn building, via the back way. Another guard—this one older and more composed—then rushed us into a small paneled waiting room next to the caucus hearing chamber.

"Wait here," Greg said. He pointed to an overstuffed couch, and by the time I had sat down and had pulled out my papers, he had disappeared into the caucus room next to us. The door remained open a crack; the hubbub next door wafted in clearly and made me nervous. It was 2:05; the hearing was scheduled for 1:45. We were late.

I looked down at my opening statement. "Mr. Chairman," it read, "members of the committee, thank you for the privilege of being able to appear here this afternoon to offer testimony concerning my activity with groups founded by Sun Myung Moon." *Moon*, I thought. To me, no longer Rev. Moon. No longer Father. Just Moon.

I had composed my statement that very morning. Greg, a research assistant for the House Subcommittee on International Organizations, had led me to believe that this would be a low-key

11

day at the hearings. But from inside the caucus room issued the clamor of a not-so-low-key crowd. Frankly, I was scared.

Well, I peeked. Curiosity and all that. And fear. You'd think that after those years in Washington, that after the Watergate hearings on TV making these rooms a national landmark, this wouldn't seem such a big thing. But in person, yes. It is a very big thing.

Peering in, I saw that the network television crews had cables and lights strewn all over the place. Funny the things you notice: the ceilings were so *high*. From my view, I couldn't see many people, but they were there—I could hear them. Smack in the middle was a table loaded with microphones. That's where I would sit.

Nearby lay a copy of that morning's *Washington Post*. The Unification Church had issued a statement that said I was "less than stable" and out "furthering my own political future." They well knew the information I had. After years of working within the Church, with Moon himself and with the president, Neil Salonen, lobbying in Washington—influence peddling—I had walked out in confusion and fear. And I carried with me a lot of information that they didn't want spread around. Even now, it hurt to think that they valued my knowledge more than they valued *me*. Where was all that *love* that had once been so alluring?

Greg was back. "They're ready," he said. "Don't worry. Just keep calm. Tell the committee everything that you have told me."

"Right," I said. Where was my voice? It sounded garbled.

"Oh, by the way," Greg said, turning back to me, "all three networks are out there. This is going to be great!" He opened the door and motioned me through.

"You're a help," I said.

Once through the door, I froze. But I wasn't so much afraid of the congressmen, seated there wearing dark suits and stern faces. I had met many of them during the course of my work. And the television paraphernalia, despite Greg's build-up, didn't really put me off. It was in the gallery. Unification Church members lined up. Moonies. Former friends. Lots of them.

Was this why everyone was so concerned for my safety?

But Greg didn't seem to notice. He grabbed my arm and helped me forward. And it seemed that the congressmen also were oblivious to the special spectators that leaned against the back walls. But *I* knew they were there.

"Do you have an opening statement, Mr. Elkins?" Congressman Frazer asked.

"Yes sir, I do," I said. The microphones picked up my voice well and boomed it throughout the caucus room.

"Mr. Chairman," I began, "members of the committee . . ."

When people are confronted by a cult, they usually want to know what it teaches: its doctrines, beliefs, the philosophy or world view that it espouses. Even here, in a House investigation, questioners groped for evidence and facts—the "what" and "where" of the problem.

But the real truth of a cult (if you can call it that)—at least its true *face*—is clearly seen only when you hold a mirror to it, when you examine its life and practice. And this is the sort of thing that can't be captured in times and places, names and dates, or theologies and Bible references. This picture of a cult begs the questions "How?" and "Why?"

Once, while I was still a Moonie, a certain thing troubled me. It had to do with a particular teaching of the Unification Church, one that emerges from the verse in Matthew where Christ says, "He who loves father or mother more than Me is not worthy of Me. . . ." Inasmuch as Moon's children are often at odds with their natural parents, the Church asserts that "to be truly principled" one must sever ties with his or her family. This teaching is stressed in a variety of ways, and it forced me to ask a question of David, a Moonie friend of mine.

I asked, "If Father asked you to do so, would you kill your mother and father for the sake of the Church?"

"In a second," David replied.

This is the fruit that a cult bears. And while it is shocking, we shouldn't be too shocked. This fruit has been cultivated over a long period of years and in our own backyard. David once had been a member of the *Christian* Church. He had lived and worshiped in our midst. We had "lost" him—probably as much through our own negligence as through the zeal of the Unification Church.

People in a hurry to condemn the Unification Church quickly latch onto this end result, this "product"—"How terrible that a young person would kill his own parents for the cause of a cult group!" (In fact, the Church would not likely ask its members to do

13

such a thing; the point is that so many Moonies would be *willing* to do it.) These people, though, fail to see the "process" that creates the "product"—that slow, almost imperceptible shifting of values, allegiances, and authority that transforms a person, even a Christian, into a member of a cult. This process is truly *subtle*, though rarely as *coercive* as some people would like to believe.

And so, when representatives and reporters asked me questions that day in September—Who? What? When? Where?—I couldn't help but think that these were the wrong questions to ask. When Christians have asked me, "Do the Moonies believe that Jesus is God?" or "Does the Unification Church think that Moon is the messiah?" I want to say that "in a way, those things don't matter so much—they don't tell the story. *How can I explain in a word or sentence all that was, for me, wrapped up in a gradual, two-and-a-half-year process?*

The term that comes closest is "deception." Heavenly deception. The policy of using falsehood to achieve, supposedly, goodness. The practice of employing lies for the sake of heaven. Heavenly deception is a thread that extends far into the fabric of the Unification Church.

I am one example. I was deceived by love. It was a complexity of thought and feeling within me that a House investigation couldn't begin to touch . . .

". . . I am ready now to answer any questions that you might have." My voice echoed throughout the caucus room. It sounded more hollow than it did when I had started. There was a silence of shuffled papers and whispers. Congressmen murmured to their aides.

I wondered if my opening statement had been sufficient. I had covered my involvement with the Church, from the beginnings in Tucson to the work in Washington and New York. I thought again of all my Moonie friends (friends?) in the gallery.

An alarm rang three times.

Congressman Frazer leaned forward and said, "We have to recess for several minutes. There's an important vote being taken on the floor of the Senate. Mr. Elkins, if you don't mind, we would appreciate your waiting until we reconvene." But I did mind. Inside I was begging them not to leave.

A question came from a *New York Times* reporter: "Are you in any physical danger, Mr. Elkins?"

Was it my imagination, or did the whole gallery lean forward to hear the answer to this one? "I think they have more to lose than to gain by harming me," I said.

True. The fear I felt wasn't a fear of physical hurt, but an irrational fear, spawned by years of dependence and blind loyalty. Even now, I dreaded some sort of spiritual retribution.

"Are there any leaders of the Unification Church present here today?" someone asked.

I had seen several from the Unification Church national head-quarters, and also various state leaders. They would love a chance for some television time. What should I do? "No," I replied, "There are none here of real importance in the Moon organization."

The questioning continued, but often I had to defer answering until the subject had been brought before the committee. Two representatives for the networks left me their cards so that I could contact them for further interviews. Then Greg stepped in and asked all the reporters to wait until after the hearing to pose their questions.

Greg winked at me reassuringly. I was doing okay. But then he had errands to run, and he slipped through the side door.

Silence. Now I wished that Greg hadn't asked the reporters to let me alone. Behind me I heard my name being whispered. Turning slightly, I saw several Moonies looking at me. Out of the corner of my eye I detected heads shaking. Some started moving down to seats closer to mine.

Had my watch stopped? Two-thirty. It seemed that it was two-thirty ten minutes ago. A hush settled into the room.

The people behind me knew me better than anyone in the whole world. I had shared more of me with them than with anyone else.

Once, we had been like brothers and sisters . . .

1

I woke up thinking about them. The alarm went off, but I was already awake. Six-thirty. For a few minutes I couldn't decide if I had dreamed the events of the night before or if they had actually happened. Singing and laughing and eating—memories still were frolicking up in my head somewhere. I had to smile just thinking about it.

There on the floor where I dropped it was the pamphlet: Divine Principle Seminar. That was proof.

"Good," I said aloud. "It wasn't a dream."

What a way for a fraternity president to spend an evening. Two and a half hours of lecture, all of it fascinating, some of it controversial, by a Dr. Shepard. Later, there was that meal. So simple, so delicious, so *enjoyable*. And, best of all, there was no booze or loud music.

"Just like my high school church youth group," I said aloud. "The fun we had."

I nearly expected my roommate, Travis, to roll over in the upper bunk and mumble, "Chris, you're talking to yourself again." Or at least a moan and then, "Chris, you don't need to shout." Travis always slept late. He always went to bed late.

But today, no Travis. Again. Wasn't this the third night in a row

17

that he hadn't come in? What was up? It worried me. Well, I knew part of what was up. I could see it in his eyes. They had seemed hazed over and distant recently.

But maybe it was just my perception of things. Perhaps Travis was acting normally. He was like others on campus—a little flaky, wandering through life casually and sedated. At the University of Arizona lots of students were like that.

Steve stopped me on the way to class. "Where's Travis?" he asked.

"Don't know," I said. "I thought you might."

Steve shrugged. Strands of his sandy-blond hair slid down over his right eye.

"What y'all do last night?"

Steve looked over at me smugly, and then a great big grin spread across his face.

"Never mind," I said. "I think I get the picture."

"I'll tell you anyway," Steve said. "Victor got some good grass from his brother—I mean really good stuff—and later we went over to Gentle Ben's for a couple beers."

"A couple?"

"Well, a few. Several." He looked over at me and started to grin again. "Well, quite a lot, really." He laughed. "How did you do last night?"

"I went to a lecture and a dinner."

"Great fun."

"It was." I sounded defensive. Steve sometimes got on my nerves. He always seemed so *taunting*.

"Sure it was," he said, feigning a yawn.

"Listen, Steve," I said. "You're not helping me with the frat house. You're supposed to help enforce the rules, not break them."

"Chris. I'm the ex-president. I make up my own rules."

"Thanks," I said sarcastically.

We had reached the front gate of campus. Normally, Steve would have gone off to the right, to Biology Lab, and I would have marched straight on, to History. But today, it was different. Across from us, about forty yards away, a column of young people walked single-file. The men were dressed in white shirts, dark pants, and thin, dark ties; the women wore dresses that were too long. They were singing and they sounded happy and confident.

The words were belted out in a sure, definite beat:

CHAPTER ONE

As the dawn breaks out of the night,
A generation will come forth.
A generation of righteousness
Coming now forth to heal the wounded land.

"Doesn't that beat all," Steve said.

We stared into the bright sun and watched them march around. They moved with the precision of a drill team, and they took no notice of the people stopping and staring at them.

The group came closer and stopped a few yards in front of the two of us. At a signal they cheered three times as if at a pep rally. And suddenly they began to pray aloud—all of them at once, loudly.

"Good grief," I muttered.

Steve shouted, "Jesus freaks!"

"Steve!" I said, turning to him. "Will you shut up?"

"What do you care?" he snapped.

"Just leave them alone. They aren't bothering you," I said.

Steve started to walk away, shaking his head. "Chris, you should have stayed in bed today. I swear, Chris. I gotta go. I'm late."

Maybe Steve was right, maybe I *was* touchy this morning. By now I was late for class, but I didn't really care. It seemed to me something more important was going on here.

"Chris! Chris!" I heard someone shout. I turned around but couldn't see very well—again, I was staring right into the sun. It was someone from the praying group. How did they know my name? The caller got closer, and then I recognized him. It was this guy I had met the day before, the one I had gone to the lecture with. Now, looking more carefully, I saw others in the group whom I recognized. Finally, I was putting it together.

"Remember me?" the caller asked. "John Shave." He spoke with a British accent. He ran up to me and embraced me as if we were long-lost brothers. When I stiffened, he pulled back and said, "Are you okay?"

Gaining my composure, I said, "Sure. I'm fine. You took me by surprise, that's all. It's awfully early in the day for surprises."

"Do you remember my friends?" John asked, waving to the group. Several of them waved back. I smiled feebly.

"I do. I do recognize some," I said. "But I'm bad at names. Say, John, I'm late for class, and I'm afraid I have to run."

"Okay," John said, smiling. "We'll see you tonight, won't we mate?"

His British intrigued me. Mate? And then I wondered what exactly he meant. "What's tonight?"

"Dr. Shepard's lecture."

"Another lecture?"

"Right-o," John said. "He's going to speak on the fall of man."

"Listen," I said. "I've got a lot to do tonight. I've got an executive council meeting at the fraternity. Look, I've got it on my schedule here, see?"

"Oh, I believe you, mate," John replied. He was still smiling. But it was as if he hadn't heard me. "I think we'll start around seven," he said. "Don't eat before you come; we'll have dinner after."

For a moment I just stood there, frozen. Across the way some of the people in the group were waving at me again.

As I turned to leave, there was Steve, standing under a tree, shaking his head and laughing.

One thing about the Moonies then (and now) was that however bizarre or eccentric their behavior might seem, a lot of their image was refreshingly normal. And consistent. Especially in places where discipline was openly flouted, where standards were trampled down, and where idiosyncracy and iconoclasm reigned, the Unification Church, with its special brand of dedication and conformity, would appear on the horizon striking and strangely sensible. And, of course, these places were often college and university campuses.

In my case, another factor that helped shed favorable light on this strange group of chanters and prayers was my relationship with Travis. He and I had grown up together in Carlsbad, New Mexico. We had gone to the same high school and we both had even become Rotary Exchange Students, although it meant that he went to Brazil, and I to New Zealand. Yet, before we left for overseas, we vowed never to lose contact with each other. We had shared good times and bad. Originally we shared the same religious convictions about Christianity. I didn't feel anything could come between us.

But at the University of Arizona things had shifted a bit. Travis was no longer sure about things. Sometimes I couldn't rely on him. The person I had looked up to and respected was now changing.

20

That Wednesday afternoon I was to meet Travis at "The Sub" at 1:15. I had managed this "appointment" with him so that we could talk some things over and get some things straight. I was worried about him. He wasn't sleeping. He looked bad.

He was already there when I arrived. He sat in a booth by a window and he was staring off into space when I walked up.

"Wake up," I said cheerfully. He jumped a little, and then chuckled nervously.

"Where have you been?" he asked.

"What do you mean? I'm on time," I said. "It's 1:15."

"Oh."

"Why, is your watch wrong?"

Travis shook his head, waved his hand vaguely at me to sit down, and muttered, "I thought you said one o'clock."

"Doesn't matter."

"Look, Chris," he said. "I don't have much time. I'm supposed to go to work an hour early this afternoon."

That meant he'd have to leave in a half hour. It aggravated me that our conversation would be rushed. Hadn't I arranged this for the very reason that we would have time to talk?

Travis, clearly, wasn't himself. He rarely forgot details; he was always on time for everything. He was always thin and sharp looking, and he always dressed on the cutting edge of fashion. But now he seemed gaunt, even a little wasted, and his clothes were wrinkled and a bit disheveled.

A waitress came up and we ordered sandwiches. A lot of silence passed between us, which usually wasn't uncomfortable, but it was today. Talk was hard.

"Are you getting enough sleep?" I asked him. His eyes looked terribly bloodshot.

"Yeah," he said. "I don't need much."

More silence. The waitress came with our sandwiches and iced teas.

"You know, Chris," Travis said, "Steve's got grass in the house."

"I figured."

"We were passing some around today. That must be why I'm so groggy. Sorry."

"You mean you were smoking it *in the house?*"

Travis cringed, but nodded. "Yeah," he replied.

"I don't know," I said, looking away. I was angry. Now even Travis was smoking grass, *in the frat house*. But, then, I didn't want to alienate Travis—I realized suddenly how much I needed him and his support—and so I let the matter drop. "I guess *every* house on campus has it now," I said.

"I guess," Travis replied.

Someone turned the jukebox on loud, making it impossible to talk. Travis, having eaten only half his sandwich, stood to leave.

"I've got to run. See you later."

Grabbing his arm, I said, "Something's wrong, Travis. Things are changing in both our lives and we're tuning each other out. Hey, let's don't let this happen."

He looked right into my eyes for a second, and I thought he opened his mouth to say something, but nothing came out. He tried to smile, then turned and walked off.

I watched him walk away. What was going on?

Suddenly, out of the corner of my eye, I saw a familiar figure sitting alone at a nearby table. John!

Was it only the day before that I had met John for the first time? In only twenty-four hours, by skirting the edges of my life, he had become a familiar, yet unnerving presence.

I had first seen John the afternoon before while sitting on the porch of the fraternity house. I was reading chapter 13 in my Economics book, and wishing that I wasn't. Those days I wasn't much enthused over anything. Studies seemed so futile. After all, what did they have to do with real life? Things were going on in the world—in Washington, in Cambodia—and I was sitting under the Tucson sun reading about microeconomics. I had ambitions to work with people; I had already been involved in politics—in the Young Republicans—but I had little time to devote to it. I was restless.

Furthermore, I was disturbed by the moral decay of life around me. It seemed that nearly everyone was stoned or crazy. Not that I was really shocked or appalled by the sex or by the drugs. I had never been so sheltered in life so that I would react *that* way. I knew about sin, in other words. But I was dismayed and disgusted. These people weren't getting anywhere; these friends of mine—fraternity *brothers* we called ourselves—weren't accomplishing anything at all.

A strange-looking guy walked toward the fraternity house. The spring in his step caught my eye. The closer he came, the more unusual he seemed. His hair was cropped short. He wore in the hot sun a long-sleeved white shirt and a black clip-on tie. Soon I realized that he wasn't walking toward the frat house, but rather toward *me*. I burrowed into my Economics text, hoping he'd go away.

Ten yards away this strange fellow stopped, extended his hand, and said in a loud voice, "Hello there, mate!"

"Hi," I said apprehensively. I walked to him and we shook hands.

Rather bluntly, and in an odd British accent, he proceeded to tell me all about an organization called the International One World Crusade. It was more than I cared to know. It wasn't *what* he said that carried weight, but instead, *how* he said it. He spoke with force and conviction. He was happy about his work.

"Why don't you come to a lecture?" he asked.

I didn't know what to say. "I'm going to be busy this evening."

"No, I mean right now. Let's go to the lecture right now."

"Now?"

"Sure, why not?" he said.

After I changed clothes, we walked across campus and chatted. Suddenly in the midst of idle conversation, he asked me about the Second Coming of Christ. We hadn't been talking theology, and the question seemed completely out of place. I tried to answer it from the knowledge I had gleaned from years of attending Sunday School in the Southern Baptist church. But, funny, I was fumbling for words; I realized how little I knew about the subject. He seemed to find this amusing.

"That's all right, mate," John said. "We'll cover it in the lecture tonight."

The confusion that began to settle in around me those days on campus was as much a distortion of *time* as anything else. Events were getting jumbled. What happened when? Had it really only been twenty-four hours since John had popped up in front of the frat house? And it seemed I knew him so well—yet, we really hadn't spent that much time together. He just kept appearing.

That Wednesday afternoon at "The Sub" I stared at the uneaten portion of Travis's sandwich, hoping that John Shave wasn't going to stop by my booth and ask me about going to the lecture.

Before long, someone was standing beside me, but it wasn't John at all; it was Alan, a frat brother. Tall and dark-haired, quiet and sensitive, Alan was a comfortable person to be around—someone I liked.

"Chris," he said, sliding into the booth across from me, "I heard you went to that lecture last night."

Oh, no, I thought. Not Alan too. Probably Steve had put him up to razzing me.

"What was it like?" Alan asked softly. He seemed to be sincere.

"You really want to know?"

"Yeah. I wouldn't ask if I didn't."

"Well, I thought it was fascinating, to be honest," I said. "Why do you care to know?"

Alan shrugged and looked away. "What was it about?" he asked.

"The Second Coming of Christ. History. Time and history. Well, you had to be there. There was a lot."

"I guess so."

"Say, Steve didn't put you up to this, did he?"

"Steve?" Alan replied. "Oh no. I haven't even seen him around."

"Well, he is around, believe me," I said. "At the wrong times and places."

"Actually, Chris, I was thinking of going tonight. I'm curious about it."

"Well, I think you should go then," I said. *Was this right? Was I advising Alan when I wasn't even sure what I should do?*

"You're Baptist, aren't you?" Alan asked.

"Yeah."

"You see, I'm Catholic."

"Oh, it doesn't matter," I said. "These people don't care what you are; they care who you are. They're very open." *Was this right? Was I really saying these things?*

"Maybe I'll see you tonight," Alan said, and he slipped out quietly and unobtrusively, the way he had come.

Sure enough, John Shave saw him leave and was standing beside me almost immediately. "Good day, mate," he chirped. "Fancy meeting you here. Do you come here often?"

"Only to eat," I said. "How about you?"

"My first visit, I do believe," he replied, looking around as if he had just entered the room. "Reminds me of some English country taverns near my home."

Realizing that he had nothing to eat, I offered him the other half of Travis's sandwich.

"No, thank you," he said. "I'm fasting, you know?" He said it as if I should know. "All I can have is water."

That's funny, I thought. Fasting? "What, then," I asked, "are you doing in a restaurant?"

John blinked at me and paused. "Uh, I guess I was—I was looking for a bathroom."

This was suspicious, I thought. I decided to press him. "By the way," I asked, "I didn't happen to see you this morning in the corridor of the Modern Languages building, did I?"

"What?"

"I could've sworn I saw you as I left class."

"I don't think so, Chris," John replied. "Say, I'd better find that bathroom." He left hurriedly, and nervously.

I sat a minute and thought. What a day this had been. And it was only 2:30. Out the window of the restaurant I glimpsed John walking away.

He hadn't even stopped at the bathroom.

2

That night at the lecture I greeted some of the people I had met there the night before—some of the same ones who had waved at me that morning as I was on my way to class. I had "brought" with me two friends, and the members of the group were all delighted.

Actually, Steve and Alan had come on their own—I didn't bring them. I had managed to postpone the time of the executive council meeting until 10:30. But when some of the guys asked why, and when I replied that I was going to a lecture and a dinner, Steve got a gleam in his eye and said, "Can I go too?"

Just then, Alan was joining us too, and I guess I was disturbed that the whole thing was going to have to be played out right there in the frat house. "Why do you want to come along?" I asked Steve harshly. "You don't even know what this is."

Steve's fat, jowly face broke into a smile. "Some of the guys say that you're going religious on us. I just want to see what this is all about. Say, Chris, all I'm trying to do is protect our frat president."

"Sure," I said. Once again I found myself having to defend a group of people that I hardly knew. I told Steve that I didn't care what he did. I thought maybe reverse psychology might win out. "Yeah, come along if you want. I don't care what you do, Steve."

He came along. So much for reverse psychology.

"Is Chris here?" someone asked, and a chill ran through me as I recognized the British accent. John, for the fourth time that day, had found me. He wanted to ensure that I had remembered the 7:00 starting time for the lecture.

The lecture was held in an ordinary classroom with harsh fluorescent lights and hard chairs. We arrived early—Dr. Shepard wasn't there yet—and I noticed that the group members effectively split up the three of us frat guys, isolating us in separate parts of the room and surrounding us with group members until Dr. Shepard stepped through the door.

Their respect for Shepard was remarkable. When he walked into the room all attention was focused on him. Everyone seemed attentive to his needs and they always, always spoke of him in glowing terms. For me, it was inspiring to see someone in authority be treated with such respect.

Jill called the meeting to order. She spoke with a British accent much like John's. (I learned later, however, that the constituency of the group is truly international.) Jill was Dr. Shepard's assistant. She exuded joy and wholesomeness as she welcomed us all. We reviewed the previous material quickly and then sang.

We sang "You Are My Sunshine" and "Onward Christian Soldiers." I had never before heard singing with such enthusiasm and gusto. I saw that Alan was fully involved and enjoying himself immensely. On the other hand, Steve was seated in the corner and was hardly participating at all. His presence was intimidating, though I don't suppose anyone else noticed him much.

While we sang, Dr. Shepard sat at the front of the room with his head bowed, praying fervently—the way that preachers sometimes prepare for special meetings or missionary services in churches or Christian rallies.

Dr. Shepard's rugged appearance reminded me a great deal of my father. They both were muscular men with dark complexions, although Shepard was shorter. Discipline seemed to be a great part of their lives. Yet, didn't I sense in Shepard a certain compassion? Shepard seemed a tender man at times. Furthermore, the whole group seemed perfectly at ease with hugging and touching and having their arms around each other. As Shepard prayed, tears sometimes would run down his cheeks. Likewise, emotion seemed a natural part of the group's existence.

Shepard spoke convincingly and logically of what he called "The

Divine Principle." He was a learned man. For over two hours he traced the fall of man in minute detail, and dug out patterns and parallels in the historical accounts that I had never thought of before. Yet I had to admit the truth of what he said. Everything was backed up by Scripture.

The story of Adam and Eve was for me that night no less intriguing and compelling than a spy thriller. And we were told that by the end we would discover one of the most startling secrets ever to be uncovered in the Bible.

Dr. Shepard explained how a man named Rev. Moon had sought and prayed to find out why man was so sinful if he was created by a God of goodness. It seemed to me to be an excellent question, one that I had asked myself many times.

Like any illness, there had to be a cause for sin, Dr. Shepard said. And once the cause was discovered a cure could be effected. Rev. Moon, we were told, had found the cause of sin and the cure was now within our reach.

While most of this sounded unfamiliar to me, it made a great deal of sense, and I was never uncomfortable with it. Certainly there was nothing said here that would pose terrific problems with my Southern Baptist church back home. Looking over at Alan, I saw that he was thoroughly engrossed in what was being said. His eyes were big with intrigue. But, Steve, scowling and sullen in the corner, wasn't buying a bit of it.

In telling us the story of the Garden of Eden, Dr. Shepard explained that our vision of Eve being tempted by a serpent with a fruit was not reasonable. We were told that the fall of man did not center on Eve's eating an apple, that these accounts had a deeper meaning, namely that the fall of man had to do with sexuality—Eve and Lucifer having a sexual relationship before Eve had one with Adam. It seemed that God wanted Adam and Eve to wait on having a family until they became spiritually and physically perfect. But Lucifer, jealous that he was not one of God's children, tried to become a child of God by having sexual intercourse with Eve. Eve realized her wrongdoing and tried to correct her sin by tempting Adam with it, since she was sure that she and Adam were intended to have a sexual relationship anyway. Adam, of course, was powerless to stave off the temptation, and thus began a family centered in Lucifer, not God.

Sin, Dr. Shepard concluded, was a genetic problem. And, sexual problems to this day are the most perverse and distorted of all sins, he told us.

"Are there any questions?" Dr. Shepard asked. One or two persons held up their hands. I looked again toward Steve and Alan. Much like myself, Alan was pondering all that he had just heard. Steve was almost laughing out loud. I found myself angry at Steve. I was very sorry that he had come with me. He was so closed-minded.

The two people that had asked questions were members of the Crusade. Having worked in politics before, I knew that questions which the speaker wanted to answer were often planted in an audience. These two questions seemed very much like that. My concentration, though, remained on Steve. Alan, too, looked irritated, and even embarrassed by Steve's laughing.

"If there are no more questions, let's close in prayer," Dr. Shepard said. As he began his prayer with "Father," everyone else in the room repeated it in passionate and subdued voices. Shepard's prayer was unusual. It was as if he was talking to someone he knew personally, someone who knew his needs and desires. Every so often, several of the members would audibly say, "Yes, Father," or simply "Father." The passion in their voices seemed sincere.

"In thy name we pray, Amen." Several of the members immediately left the room. John, though, stayed with me, and a couple of other members stayed with Alan. Steve now was nowhere to be seen. Dr. Shepard came to me and in a very fatherly way put his arm around my shoulders. "Let's go get something to eat," he said, and he motioned the others to come with us.

Outside, we all climbed into a Dodge van. I had no idea where we were going. Still discussing the lecture, the members asked Shepard questions which he answered with assurance and authority. I listened, but did not ask questions. Alan was talking to Linda, a rather heavy-set girl who had joined the group a few weeks earlier in Phoenix. They were laughing and kidding with each other, and, I noticed, it seemed to disturb Dr. Shepard. Catching a motion of his eyes, two members walking near Shepard dropped back and tactfully broke up the levity. That struck me as being odd, but I did not question Dr. Shepard's authority or intentions. He knew what was best.

In the van Shepard sat in the passenger seat next to the driver.

Once inside, everyone bowed and said a silent prayer. For a few minutes there was no sound at all.

"Let's go," Shepard said to the driver, which seemed to signal the end of the prayer. Noticing the puzzled look on my face, Dr. Shepard explained that they always ask God to be with them whatever it was they were doing. "Satan can attack at any time, so we must always enlist God's presence to protect us." I was impressed with their desire to bring God into all matters.

On our van trip to the "Center" I asked Shepard why they had sung and prayed on campus that first morning I saw them. Without the least bit of hesitation he told me they had made a condition with God. Shepard said they viewed the walled-in campus at the university as an impregnable fortress. To them it was like the biblical city of Jericho, which fell after the Israelites marched and prayed around it seven days.

"God will bless our efforts if we show him that we are serious and really want to win people from the campus to him. So we promised him we would sing and pray each morning like the Israelites did."

Alan sat beside me and did not say a word. After Shepard's comment he looked at me in a daze and said, "These people are saints." Speechless, I just looked at him and nodded.

The Center was about ten blocks from the main gate of the campus. We pulled into the driveway of a rather old but neatly kept house. As we got out, Shepard explained that this house was only a temporary place to stay until they could find a more permanent center. I was startled to find it devoid of any furniture. Alan and I stood motionless as everyone who entered bent over and took off his shoes. Realizing that we were expected to do the same, Alan and I took ours off too. Dr. Shepard and all the male members of the Crusade disappeared into a room on the left and the women went upstairs.

"The rest of us are back here," a voice boomed out from the right. We walked through an empty room, which I assumed to be a living room, and into another room behind it. It must have been the dining room because of its proximity to the kitchen. But still, we found no furniture. Instead there were about ten people sitting on the floor around the room. They looked exhausted and some were very sunburned. The moment Alan and I entered the room, they all jumped up to greet us.

31

The booming voice belonged to Rob Kittle. He was the only one who did not get up, and I noticed that his feet were bandaged. Rob was at least six and a half feet tall and was built like a football player. He gave me the impression of being gentle as a bear. He smiled from one ear to the other as he asked me to sit beside him.

I noticed that for the first time that evening John was not at my side. Alan had already sat down with a couple of other people, so I sat with Rob.

I noticed that most of the people in the room were those who left the lecture immediately after the prayer. I asked where Steve was. With a nervous glance, a girl across the room replied, "We dropped him off at your fraternity house. He didn't seem to understand us as well as you and Alan do." Deep inside I was glad to know that he would not be around for the rest of the evening.

I could smell food from the kitchen. I asked Rob what was cooking. He laughed and said, "I don't know for sure, but Rosemary's fixing it and she's a great cook. I'm sure it'll be good." About that time a red-haired, freckled girl entered the room from the kitchen.

"Hello, Chris," she said, rolling the r in my name, typical of her Scottish brogue. "I'm Rosemary. I hope you like shepherd's pie." Everyone in the room voiced their approval. I hadn't had shepherd's pie since I had been in New Zealand three years earlier. It brought back pleasant memories.

Just then Dr. Shepard came into the room and asked Rob about his bandaged feet. With obvious embarrassment Rob looked down as he explained what had happened.

"I made a condition with God to let me find a new member today while I was witnessing on campus. I ran around the courtyard three times in bare feet to show God that I was willing to suffer in order to find someone." Thinking about how hot the concrete gets in the middle of one of Tucson's 100 degree-plus days made my feet ache. What a passionate gesture, I thought. Rob, though, still hung his head.

Then, in a near-rage Dr. Shepard yelled, "You let Satan invade your witnessing! God would not expect such a stupid thing from you. I am sure your feet are so blistered now that you won't be able to walk for days. Satan has stopped your witnessing." He turned to the other members and barked, "You are not to make conditions without my approval. You are all young in your faith, and Satan can

32

easily invade even the best of your intentions." He then turned back to Rob. "Go read the Principle and then pray to God for forgiveness. You must rid yourself of Satan."

Dr. Shepard was red in the face as Rob pulled to his feet and struggled to leave the room. I stood to help him, but Dr. Shepard said, "Sit down, Chris. He must fight off Satan by himself." In shock I sat back down. Everyone in the room was tense. Alan and I were scared.

But as quickly as he had gone into a fury, Dr. Shepard mellowed. He smiled and said, "Let's entertain our guests before dinner." With child-like glee all the members jumped up as if the preceding scene had not occurred. Alan and I sat still, almost dumbfounded by the quick change of mood. I looked at Alan and smiled in disbelief. He shrugged his shoulders and we, too, began to join in the mood again.

Two of the girls sang a duet while another played the guitar. We all then sang a round and joined hands to sing "We Shall Overcome." At that point Rosemary asked us to come into the kitchen. Dinner was served smorgasbord style, and everyone insisted that Alan and I eat first.

John did not eat, I noticed, which was reassuring to me. At least his fasting was on the level. He motioned for me to sit by him as I came out of the kitchen. Alan followed closely and sat on the other side of me. Dr. Shepard was the next one out of the kitchen. He motioned for Alan to scoot over so he could sit between us. Dr. Shepard paused and prayed before he began to eat, as did all of the other members as they made their way into the dining room.

I noticed that it was almost ten-thirty and I remembered the executive council meeting back at the house. They couldn't start without me. I hurriedly finished my meal and explained to Dr. Shepard that I had to leave. Alan said he needed to go, too. Every member of the group got up and walked with us to the front gate where they sang a short song to us. We noticed tears in the eyes of some. After bidding goodnight, Alan and I walked back to the fraternity house.

We walked in silence, staring straight ahead. Somehow, words were out of place.

Thursday
June 18, 1973
Tucson, Arizona

It was 3:20 A.M. I woke out of a deep sleep to see a tall, shadowy figure standing beside my bed. It startled me, and I jerked straight up, saying, "Who's there?" banging my head on the top bunk.

It was Alan. He bent over to see if I had hurt myself.

"Chris. Are you all right?" he said softly.

"Yeah. I'm okay," I said. "What're you doing?"

"Sorry. I didn't mean to be a bother."

"It's all right, Alan," I said. "But what's up?"

"I can't sleep. The meeting. The events keep playing over and over in my head like a tape loop or something."

"Yeah. I know."

"It's fascinating stuff," Alan said, still whispering. "But, you know something? It scares me. It scares me, Chris."

Alan knelt down beside me and continued. "I felt myself drawn to them. Like you said, they're warm, easy people. I could let myself be myself—no facades."

I sat up in my bed and propped a pillow in back of me. We started talking in low, hushed tones. The cold light of the moon shafted through the open window and washed half of Alan's face in a cool glow.

"What did you think of the lecture?" he asked.

"Well—" I started to say.

"It made sense in terms of logic," he went on, "but, at times, I felt

35

like a cat being petted in the wrong direction."

I nodded. I had felt the same thing. "But, you know, this business about the fall of man being derived from a sexual thing makes a lot of sense to me. Maybe it explains the sexual confusion of the world today."

We fell silent, thinking. Funny, we weren't tired. Just talking about it was invigorating.

I said, "'Judge a tree by its fruits.' My preacher back home always said that. The fruit of this tree is love and discipline. It looks good to me, Alan."

"I don't know the Bible very well," he said.

"Well, I'm beginning to think that I don't either. These people find things in the Scriptures I never knew were there. Yet, I can't refute it. But I've been going to church all my life. I *ought* to know this stuff."

"I keep coming back to this one thing—love. Chris, tonight these people *loved* me. It was *real*."

"Yeah," I said. "I know."

"Doesn't the Bible say that God is love?" Alan asked.

"Somewhere," I replied.

Alan grinned. "Well thanks, Chris. I just wanted to know what you were thinking."

I reached over and put my arm around his shoulder. "That's all right. I'm as confused as you are. Maybe we can help each other through this thing."

"If one of our frat brothers saw you put your arm around me like that, they might think something strange."

"Who cares?" I said indignantly. "These guys—Alan, a lot of people around here could learn a little something about love."

Alan nodded in agreement.

"Goodnight," I said.

"Goodnight, Chris," Alan replied. "Thanks."

But it wasn't much of a night for sleep. Just as I started to doze off, I thought I heard a voice. "Chris," someone called distantly. It seemed like the opening of a dream. But there it was again.

"Chris."

This time the voice was audible and definable. It was Travis on the upper bunk.

CHAPTER THREE

I turned over on my back and said, "I didn't know you were up there."

"I came in a bit earlier."

"Oh," I said. I wondered if he had been asleep.

"I heard you and Alan," Travis said. "I didn't mean to overhear, but it was kind of hard to miss it."

"I guess so," I said. I didn't know what Travis would think. Recently, he had not been too concerned about religious matters, and I didn't think this business of lectures and fellowship dinners and the International One World Crusade would set with him very well. And Travis's opinion mattered to me a great deal. I had always sought his approval for what I did.

"Chris, I'm sorry if I've been putting you off," he said.

"That's okay," I replied cautiously.

"It sounds as if you've found something special."

He was fishing for information, I could tell. Now, at just the time *he* wanted to talk, I wasn't sure that *I* wanted to. "I've been wanting to tell you about it," I said.

"I guess I've been gone a lot these days. Maybe you just haven't had the chance."

"I guess not." I paused. There it was, 3:45 A.M., everything bursting to come out, yet it wasn't the right time. "You know, it's really gotten to Alan," I said.

"And you too?" Travis asked.

"Listen," I said, "these people are not just a bunch of emotional freaks. They use their heads. Travis, they're your kind of people. Some of the things they're saying just boggles the mind."

"Maybe I should come to one of the lectures," Travis said.

"Maybe you should."

"What about tonight?"

"Fine," I said.

"And maybe we can talk after, huh?"

"Sounds fine," I said. Inside, I was bubbling over. Travis was going to do the two things I wanted him to do—all in the same day. I felt good.

"Are you tired?" Travis asked me.

I laughed. "You bet. What a night. Are you tired?"

"No, not really," Travis replied. "Not really."

Hindsight gives you wisdom about past events—a wisdom you didn't have when the events occurred. It's an unfair advantage to look back and say, with the confidence of a retrospective, "I should've done this," or "I should've seen this particular thing going on."

Certainly, though, my increasing involvement with Dr. Shepard and his obedient, loving children was at the time a perfectly logical direction to take. Given the knowledge I had at the time, given the joy and love being expressed to me then, and given the creeping disillusionment that was sneaking into my consciousness about the nature of university life, and for all I knew, life in the society outside—my steps made sense.

But I wish I had had the wisdom to see what was happening to Travis. Perhaps if I had not been so wrapped up in myself I might have seen that the disintegration of my best friend was not only itself a tragedy, but represented the disintegration of many—the slow disengagement with social issues and the gradual preoccupation with self and spiritual questions. It was the malaise of the seventies. Travis and I were both traveling in it—on different trains.

That day, Thursday, the day of the third lecture, I discovered that Travis was moving out of the frat house. He assured me that we would still be good friends, "close as ever." He mentioned something about things that he wanted to try. He didn't name them, but I thought I knew what they were. He said that he didn't want me to desert him. It was (although then I didn't perceive it as such) a call for help.

Maybe I "listened" to Travis say all these things, but what I "heard" was only that he was moving out. Travis had been an anchor in my life. He kept me objective and honest and close to reality. Now, he made me feel cut off. This guy was my friend—perhaps my only *real* friend at the time. I was hurt, and it was all I could do to keep from crying.

Thursday night I was late for the lecture, and as I came close to the classroom I could hear that the group had already started to sing. The voices I heard were familiar and I eagerly walked up to the door.

But suddenly I heard Steve's voice singing above the rest. I stopped dead in my steps. I heard the mockery in his voice. And when his laugh rang out I knew he was making light of the proceedings.

It made me sick enough to go to the men's room. There, I stared at myself in the mirror. I felt nauseated and tense, and I had the greatest desire to turn and run out of the building and get as far away as possible. I knew that if I went back to the classroom, I'd have to choose sides.

I stared deeply into my own eyes in the mirror. I said to myself, "Chris, you can't please everyone. You have to get on one side or the other. Running won't help. You have to face it." It was as if I were choosing between good and evil.

Then suddenly my nausea was gone. Quickly, not giving myself a chance to change my mind, I raced once again to the classroom.

When I burst into the room, all eyes turned to me. Dr. Shepard was leading the singing. He looked right at me and said, "I knew you would come. We have been fighting Satan for you."

That puzzled me, and I didn't know what he meant, but I didn't think much about it at the time. I saw Steve now, in the corner, subdued and almost reverent. To Dr. Shepard I said, "Thanks," and I sat down beside John. They had been waiting for me. It was good to know that I was important to them.

The lecture that night was on history. About halfway through Travis stepped in and sat down. That made it terribly hard for me to concentrate. With Steve scowling in the back, Alan over to the side listening intently, and now a curious Travis sitting near the door, I didn't hear much of what Dr. Shepard was saying.

The lecture was long that evening and Travis had to leave before it was over. As he left he glanced at me and flashed a wink and a smile which were as good as saying that he approved. Alan, catching Travis's expression, looked over at me and grinned. Suddenly things felt a lot better.

Dr. Shepard, later that night, asked me to call him Joseph. I should feel free to call on him if I had any more needs, he said. I told him of my "battle of spirit" earlier that evening, and he replied that he knew all about it and he identified the culprit as Satan. He said that Satan would do all that he could to keep me from God, that he would even use the people I was closest to, and that I should be prepared.

That night when I got to my room a light was on and Steve was sitting beside my bed. He was reading my Bible. Just the sight of him there made me furious. I walked in, slammed the door, and scared him, quite visibly.

"Guy! What are you doing? You scared me to death. What do you mean sneaking up behind me like that?"

"It's only my room, Steve," I said coolly. "What do you think you're doing here?"

"Reading your Bible," he said, composing himself.

"That's quite noble, but I'd appreciate it if you'd ask my permission before you barged in and started using my things."

"You know, Chris, I was just looking up some of the things those people quoted tonight." He spoke so smugly and condescendingly. "They sure use the Bible a lot. But I can't find some of their quotes, though."

Steve's presumption and cockiness set me on edge. "Get out," I said.

He smiled that jowly smile again. "I'm just trying to protect you from the clutches of Satan," he said.

"I can make my own decisions," I said. "Get out."

For the next three days Steve, Alan, and I attended the lectures. Alan and I grew more enamored of the Crusade as Steve grew more and more disgusted. Every night after the lectures Steve would pace through the house raving, almost like a madman, about the subtle evil he perceived in the movement.

The last three lectures were on Christology and the Last Days. These were delivered to only the three of us, with no one else present. At one point Joseph made the statement that Jesus had not completed his mission on earth. This sent Steve into a rage. And while I did not exactly agree with Joseph either, I couldn't at all identify with Steve's attitude. After all, if God is love, then God's people will be loving. The last thing I saw in Steve was love.

On the evening of the last lecture Joseph asked to see Alan and me alone. He told us that the last lecture would be the most revealing yet. Through all of this I had noticed that Alan was visibly embarrassed by Steve's outbursts and ridicule of the movement on campus. Alan would duck out of conversations in which the movement was brought up. Toward the end, I thought that Alan would slip away from the whole thing, but he continued to attend the lectures faithfully.

The fraternity had planned a swim party for the same afternoon that Joseph had wanted to see Alan and me specially. When Joseph

40

asked us about coming, I immediately said yes, but Alan would not commit himself.

Joseph looked squarely at Alan and said, "The powers of Satan will do anything to keep you from hearing this last lecture. If you hear it, it will change your life. If Satan can keep you from coming, you have miserably failed God. Now, what is more important? Going to a swim party or doing God's will?"

To my surprise Alan held his ground. He said, "My commitment to God is between God and myself. No one else interprets it for me. No one intimidates me about it." He spoke these words surely and softly, and then he walked away.

But tears welled up in Joseph's eyes. "I wish I could help him," he said. "You and Alan did not find God. God found you. Right now I feel the heartbreak that God must feel over his disobedient children. Alan could do so much for God, but he is being rebellious."

Joseph grabbed me by the shoulders and looked directly into my eyes. "Chris," he said to me, "you have been the only positive response that we have gotten from this campus. I feel that God has sent us here just to find you. You must be very special to God. Don't fail him. Please don't fail him."

There was a deep silence as we looked at each other. I thought how wonderful a servant of God Joseph was. He cried over the lost ones, and his love tempered all of his emotions.

I looked up into his eyes and said, "Joseph, I won't fail."

Joseph's last lecture was on the Second Coming of Christ. I was his only pupil. Steve had dropped out in disgust. Alan had left quietly. I missed Alan's presence, but I was determined to carry it through.

Joseph was a good teacher. He spoke to me sensibly and logically. There were no emotional hysterics, no artificial kinds of manipulation, no attempts at psychological browbeating. Joseph was fond of the Socratic method. He made his points by asking questions and by a strict, relentless logic—a characteristic of the lectures that had appealed to me.

"Chris," he asked me, "do you think you'll be aware of Christ's Second Coming when it happens?"

Warily, I replied, "Yes, I believe that I will."

"Could it have already happened and maybe you missed it?" Joseph asked with a glint in his eye.

"No—or at least I don't think so."

"So, you feel prepared for Christ's coming, right?"

"Yes," I answered.

"For a moment," Joseph said, "let's imagine that you and I lived 2000 years ago at the time when Jesus first came. If we had been Jews then I am sure that we would have been prepared for the advent of the messiah. Yet, imagine if one of your Jewish friends would have come up to you and told you that he thought that a

43

Nazarene carpenter was the Christ. What would have been your reaction?"

I sat in silence shaking my head. His point was all too clear.

"Do you think that you would have accepted Christ? Or would you have been like the vast majority who rejected him? After all, Jesus did not come as the king that the Jews expected. Yet, the Jews had been prepared for the coming of Christ. They had been living for the day. Most of them missed it."

We sat in silence for a few minutes. Then Joseph continued, "Today most Christians are prepared for Christ's return. Yet, isn't it possible that they too could miss it as the Jews did?"

I wanted to say no, but I didn't know how to defend my answer. He sounded so logical.

"We know that Christ will come out of the East. It tells us that in the Book of Revelation. But will he come to us in the clouds, or will he return in an unexpected way? Maybe the clouds are just symbolic."

To my naive mind, this all made sense. My curiosity began to rise and I began to see his point.

In the lectures we had been taught the history of the Old Testament. We had been shown, through charts and diagrams not unlike those found in the back of certain Bibles or those preached from certain pulpits, how that history fell into patterns. One of these patterns concerned the idea that God had sent to earth a divine messenger approximately every 1,914 to 1,927 years. There was Moses and there was Elijah and then Jesus . . . .

Jesus was born in A.D. 3 or 4. What Joseph was saying now indicated to me that if a messiah were to be sent in our age he likely would have been born between A.D. 1917 and 1930—3 plus 1,914 or 1,927.

Furthermore, we had been taught that the return of Elijah which the prophet Malachi had foretold (Malachi 4:5) was really the person of John the Baptist (Mark 1:2, Malachi 3:1). John assumed the mission of Elijah, but not the same body and physical appearance. Why couldn't a new messiah return in the same manner?

Suddenly, Joseph was not asking questions anymore but making statements that he considered foregone conclusions.

"If Christ was born in the East between 1917 and 1930 he must be

44

alive today. What could be more important than knowing him? It is like living at the time of Jesus. Knowing and following Christ is the most important thing that anyone could do," Joseph said with excitement in his voice.

"But who is he?" I asked curiously. "Surely you would not have brought me this far and not be able to tell me who he is."

Joseph smiled. "Chris, this is something that you must discover for yourself. All I can tell you is that God has given us the keys to discover the answers. We know that he must be coming from the East. Since God always sends his messenger to those prepared, we must find a group of prepared people in the Orient."

"Christians?" I asked.

"Right. Where in the East are there the most Christians?"

In my missions study as a Royal Ambassador I had studied Korea and I knew it to be the country in the East with greatest percentage of Christian population. "Korea," I answered.

He smiled, but did not say whether I was right or wrong. "If Christ was born on earth between 1917 and 1930 then he is at most sixty-six years old, or as young as forty-three," Joseph explained. "And, if he is that old, then he most likely would have a worldwide mission organization. And one other distinguishing feature: like all of God's messengers he will be rejected and persecuted in his own time."

I summed it up. If I had followed Joseph correctly, then there would have to be a middle-aged Korean man with a worldwide mission organization, one who experiences persecution and rejection, who is the Christ. At first I drew a blank. Then I recalled Joseph telling me about a man he had a picture of in his lecture notes. He had called the man "Reverend Moon" and had told me that he was a Korean. I had also noticed that John carried a small picture of Reverend Moon in his coat pocket. When I had asked John who that was, he replied, "Oh, this is someone that will grow to be more important in your life a little later on."

Joseph had not said anything for several minutes as I rolled all of this over in my mind. I looked at Joseph and asked, "Is Reverend Moon the one? I mean is he the Christ?"

Joseph paused a few seconds. As if weighing each word carefully, he answered, "Chris, pray to God and ask him. I cannot tell you. After all, in Matthew it tells us to believe no one who says, 'Lo, there is the Christ.'"

That didn't satisfy me. "But, Joseph," I asked, "do *you* believe that Reverend Moon is the Christ?"

He grinned from ear to ear. "Chris," he said, "if I told you what I believed then you may want to believe because I do. I don't want to be responsible for your decision. Why don't you go pray about it and come back in an hour or two?"

Without saying another word, I simply stood up, looked at Joseph inquisitively, and left. I wanted to go talk to someone about it, but who would understand me? My parents? They would surely think I was crazy. Travis? He would think that it was too religious. Alan? No, he had not heard that final lecture yet, and I would spoil it for him. Anyhow, he was probably at the swim party.

In some ways I was overcome with excitement at just the possibility of being on the inside of something great. I began to think that this was how Matthew, Mark, or Luke must have felt as they discovered the identity of Jesus. Surely they had doubts too, I thought to myself.

I pulled up to the tennis courts so I wouldn't have to concentrate on driving. The love of the One World Crusade members had been enough to convince me that God was with them. Their lectures seemed so biblically based. Yet, the conclusion was scary. If Moon was the Christ, what would be my next step? Would I have to follow? Would I become a "disciple?"

But, suddenly, I realized that no one had asked me to join the group anyway. I had discovered that most of the Crusade members had college degrees and seemed to know their theology well. I often felt like a simpleton around them. "They might not even ask me to join," I said to myself out loud. The thought crushed me. They might decide that I wasn't good enough. I began to fear their rejection so badly that I found myself scheming to get their acceptance.

When I got back to the Center, Steve's car was out front. It almost spoiled my desire to go in, but I knew that my friends there would help me overcome his attacks. Rosemary met me at the door and asked me to go back into the kitchen with her. "Joseph is presenting the conclusions to Steve," she said in her quaint Scottish accent. "He should be finished soon."

"Why is Joseph wasting his time on Steve? Isn't his attitude obvious to all of you?" I asked resentfully.

"Chris," Rosemary said, rolling the *r* in my name, "God's love is meant for everyone. Even Steve. We don't understand his attitude, but God has changed all of us and we know he can change Steve, too."

I was embarrassed. My attitude was so jaded in comparison to hers. Her unconditional love for Steve made even more of a believer out of me.

"What does Rev. Moon mean to you?" I asked her.

She quickly turned and faced me. Holding a freshly baked pie in her hands, she tried to appear calm as she answered. "He is a great man," she said. "I heard him speak recently, and his inspiration and love are wonderful." Her carefully selected words did not commit her to a stand about Moon's Christhood. No one was giving me a straight answer.

Maybe they really don't know, I thought. Surely, if they believed he was the Christ, they would be bold enough to admit it.

At that moment I heard Steve's voice ring out. "I knew it! I knew that you believed that Moon is the Christ. It had to be. That explains your devotion and these intense feelings. This is the most un-Christian thing I have ever heard. You have denied the lordship of Jesus Christ; you have called him and John the Baptist failures, yet you call yourself Christians. This is a mockery! Moon is an antichrist!"

Rosemary watched every expression on my face. I could tell she was trying to say something to soothe me, but I just smiled at her as if Steve's outburst meant nothing to me.

At that point Steve and Joseph both came into the kitchen. When Steve saw me he snapped, "I suppose that you have heard these preposterous conclusions. Didn't I tell you that they were satanic? These people are following an antichrist."

"Steve," I said, "wasn't Jesus accused of deriving his powers from Beelzebub? Didn't people think that Jesus was a false prophet in his own time?"

"You're being taken in by this," Steve said. "You still believe it! Chris, come to your senses."

Steve didn't know it, but he was playing into their hands. I had already been told that one sign that God was in this movement is that friends would accuse you and desert you. Joseph had not said a word of defense during the whole scene. Yet, the way he looked at me spoke clearly: "I told you so."

I stood there silently as Steve headed for the door. "C'mon," he said, "let's go talk this over." His face was red with anger.

I had to make a choice. It was an almost symbolic one. If I went with Steve, then I endorsed him. If I stayed with Joseph then I endorsed the Crusade. I didn't move. Steve, in great disgust, stormed out the door.

"Satan isn't being very subtle in Steve," Joseph said.

"I have prayed for him so much," Rosemary added. "What a victory for God he would be."

"I'm just glad that you guys are here. I don't know how much longer I can handle him."

The door opened behind me, and fearing that it was Steve returning for revenge, I cowered as I turned. To my surprise, in walked several of the other Crusade members. They were startled by my reaction.

"Are you all right?" Rob asked me.

"Yeah," I said. "I thought it was Steve coming back."

"We saw him leaving," Rob said with a chuckle. "Boy, was he angry."

"How did you do?" Joseph asked.

Rob replied with a little hesitation, "We were kicked out of one place and it took time to find another good area. We didn't make as much as we wanted to."

"Then you should not have come back," Joseph replied. "Father will be greatly disappointed in you."

I wondered who "Father" was. And I also wondered where Rob and the others had been. Since they were all a little sunburned I assumed they had been outside.

Joseph, perceiving my confusion, answered only one of my questions. "They've been out fund raising today. That's how we support ourselves."

"You mean you sell things in parking lots?" I asked.

"Sure," Joseph answered. "This way we spend only one day each week raising the financial needs of our life-style. The other days we witness for God."

As usual, we sang a few songs before we ate. Everyone's face had a bright, cheerful quality about it. Although the group was fatigued, there seemed to be in their faces the satisfaction that goes with a hard, but highly rewarding day.

"Chris," Joseph said. "Why don't you sing a song?"

I instantly started stammering, trying to find an excuse. The whole group encouraged me and begged me to sing.

"I don't know what song to sing," was my weak reply. I had been in several choirs while in high school and college, but I had never been a soloist.

Joseph picked up a song book and thumbed through it. "Brother," Joseph said, referring to me, "you have been quite fond of a song we sing a lot. Why don't you sing it to us? 'The Judgment Song.'"

I was fond of it, but I had sung it with the group each time and wasn't familiar enough with the tune to sing a solo. Again, though, everyone cheered me on.

"Chris," Joseph said authoritatively, "sing!"

Since I had little choice at that point, I began to sing. The rhythm of the song was syncopated, which made it even harder for me. Everyone clapped as I sang:

> *Gather 'round*
> *Give ear everybody,*
> *Listen to what the Lord has to say.*
>
> *Stop your shoutin'*
> *And cease from cryin',*
> *We're livin' in the Judgment Day.*
>
> *Sun flashing in his swirling sword,*
> *Torn from cold, dead stone.*
> *As the cosmic dawn approaches,*
> *And men all come back home.*

At that point everyone joined in with me and helped me finish singing. They all smiled so lovingly at me and Joseph put his arm around me as we sang the rest of the song. I felt as if I was part of a large family.

Never in my life had I heard such heart-felt singing. They really did feel good about being alive.

Joseph, with his arm around me, said, "Family, we have a new brother."

5

I had *not* made the decision to join. I had told no one that I even wanted to. Joseph had assumed that when I had stepped into the classroom that Saturday evening, it was tantamount to a full-term commitment. Since there was so much joy, and since such overwhelming acceptance immediately dashed my fears that I might be rejected because I wasn't smart or capable enough, I said nothing to stop all the celebration. I did nothing to keep them from taking me in.

Still, I had my doubts.

This is the point of various misconceptions about the Unification Church. For one thing, it is often thought that induction into a cult comes about as a result of intellectual conviction. At least in my case this was not true. I doubted plenty, but I was thoroughly convinced of this group's sincerity and love. For another thing, I did not at this time perceive this group as a "cult." To me, it was a group of Christians. In fact, I was not even that familiar with the name "Unification Church." I identified the group as the International One World Crusade. Even the Rev. Moon had not been until lately a dominant figure in our discussions.

51

In the days that followed I was plunged in turmoil about the movement, about my life, about morality, and most of all, about what it meant to be Christian. Christ, of course, is our example of exemplary living and servanthood; the only people I knew who truly lived in the manner of Christ were my friends at the Center: Joseph, John, Rosemary, Rob, and the others.

At one point I asked Joseph, "Am I supposed to move into the Center?"

Joseph replied, "This is a time of struggle, a war against Satan. We need every man to give his all in order to win the battle. Living in the Center will help you grow closer to God and also help you answer your questions. With you here, you are readily available to God. If you live elsewhere, then you are more likely to be drawn away by Satan."

I had mixed emotions about moving in. It would mean a real loss of personal freedom. "What about the fraternity, Joseph?" I asked.

"Is God working through your fraternity to build the kingdom of heaven on earth?" he asked in answer to my question.

"But, Joseph, I'm president of it."

"In the Bible the rich man would not give up his earthly possessions to follow Jesus. Is there anything more valuable than eternal life?"

"I think you must have an answer for everything," I said with a smile on my face.

"No, Chris," Joseph replied, "I don't. But I know someone who does!"

Everything he said always seemed to have a deeper meaning beyond its apparent meaning. But sometimes I just couldn't figure it out.

That night I slept on a cot out on the frat house porch. It was hot inside, and also strangely stifling. Suddenly, the fraternity didn't seem as inviting as it once had.

I hadn't been sleeping long when I heard my name called. "Chris."

It was Alan. "We need to talk again," he said. "I'm sorry to wake you. I pick the oddest times."

"It's okay," I said. "Maybe we should start a little 2:00 A.M. discussion group." I sat up in the cot and looked out into the night. "Really," I said, "it's okay. It's a fine evening."

"We've gone through a lot in the last week," he said.

"Yes, we have."

"The pressure got to be too much for me. I admire you, Chris. Somehow you've withstood all the harassment. Steve doesn't seem to have affected you. I'm just not that strong."

"Hey, wait a sec," I said quickly. "I've been as ruffled as you have been. It's just this disguise I'm wearing."

Alan smiled. "Well, at any rate, I can see that you're going to make a great commitment and that it will entail great sacrifice. It's not that I don't want the commitment, but I can't bring myself to accept the sacrifice."

"Alan," I blurted out, "it's hard for me, too. If there weren't so much to gain, I couldn't do it either." Just then I remembered that Alan had missed the last lecture. That was the difference. He hadn't heard about the Rev. Moon.

A fresh breeze blew over the porch. We were quiet for awhile, but I sensed that Alan had more to say. The Arizona sky was packed with stars and just a sliver of a moon. It was a good night, an important night.

I said, "You need to hear the last part of the lecture series. It could change your mind."

Alan looked down at his hands and then out at the stars and the blue-black sky. "Steve told me about the conclusions. Frankly Chris, I don't see how you can accept the notion of a Korean Messiah."

Steve again. Steve. It riled me that Steve had spoiled it for Alan. "Steve drew that conclusion himself," I said loudly.

"But—"

"I have yet to hear one person in the Crusade say that they believe that," I stated firmly. "And I have asked them."

"Chris, my faith won't even allow me the *possibility* of a Korean Messiah."

His faith, I thought, was nonexistent until he needed it for an excuse to avoid committing himself to something. "Alan," I said, "many a prepared Jew missed the Christ 2000 years ago because their faith would not allow them to accept a Nazarene carpenter. I have not accepted Moon as the Christ, but I *have* accepted the thought that I don't know enough about what I believe and that I need to do some exploring."

My voice has a way of sounding angry when it gets excited. I wasn't angry at Alan, but I was afraid that maybe he thought I was. "Hey," I said. "I'm not mad. But I'll be disappointed if you don't give

53

yourself the opportunity to really know the truth. Promise me you'll hear that last lecture. It could make all the difference."

"I can't do that, Chris."

"Why not?"

"Let me sleep on it, okay?"

"Sure," I said. "I have a big decision to make tomorrow too. We could use the rest."

I don't remember him leaving. My mind was preoccupied by questions: Was I going to move into the Center? Could I make all the sacrifices that would be required of me?

Later that day I submitted this letter to the Executive Council of the fraternity:

> Brothers of Phi Sigma Kappa,
> Commitment is one of the greatest requirements expected out of us as fraternity brothers. It yields the greatest rewards as well. As your president I can only tell you that the requirements of commitment are primary to all others as I try to serve you.
> In recent days I have made other commitments that conflict with those I have to you. In order that you might be served best I hereby submit my resignation as president and active member, to be effective immediately. Our bylaws require that our vice president assume the presidency. I wish you well in your endeavors.
>
> Sincerely,
> Chris D. Elkins

Later that day the national president of our fraternity, Dick Stribling, phoned long distance. It was a curious call. Our chapter, being one of the smaller ones, rarely heard from the national office, especially by phone.

I had to walk by Steve in order to get to the phone. He didn't even look up.

"Good to hear from you, Dick," I said.

"How are you?" he asked.

"Just fine." This was puzzling. Why would Dick be calling just now?

"I just wanted to express our support of the work you are doing out there. We've heard good things about your leadership."

Finally, I was putting it together. This was not just a spontaneous, friendly call of encouragement, but rather a call that had been carefully orchestrated by Steve. It was a last-ditch effort to keep me from joining the Crusade.

"I hate to be the bearer of bad news, Dick," I said, "but I've just resigned as president."

There was a moment's silence. Then, "Why Chris, you can't do that!"

"What do you mean?" I asked.

"You can't resign."

"Sure I can," I said. "I just did and the executive council just accepted it."

"What about your oath?"

"Service to God," I said, "comes before all service."

"Chris, I'm going to fly out and talk this thing over with you."

"Dick, that's not necessary. I've made up my mind."

"You sound pretty far gone," Dick replied. I detected sarcasm in his voice and I didn't mean to have any of it.

"Well," I said, "I'm sorry you feel that way. Thanks for the call. I've got to go," I said, hanging up before I heard his comment.

I turned to see Steve standing right behind me. His face was so red that I thought blood would ooze from it. "Get out of here, you fool," he shouted at me.

"You have no right—" I started to say.

"You are such a waste," he said vehemently. "I've done my best to help you and to show you that they are wrong. But you've buried yourself with them, and I hope that you rot!"

I ran past Travis on my way out.

I told him that I was moving out, and that I was joining the Crusade. "Those people in that house have turned on me," I said, "especially Steve."

Travis immediately absorbed the gravity of the situation. "Chris," he said, "don't go off mad. That's no good. You aren't mad at me, are you?"

"No," I said. "But just now I needed you. You weren't there."

He looked away and I could tell that I had hurt him deeply.

"But," I continued, "I haven't been around to help you either, have I?"

Travis smiled weakly and shook his head. "I'm going to get some sleep. Why don't you stop by and see me before I go to work?"

"Okay," I said. "I'll try. Right now I've got to get out of here." I turned and walked off. I felt a little better. I knew inside that Travis was still the best friend I had.

"Let me fill you in on a few things, Chris, since you will be living with us," Joseph said. "First of all, we do not date or have any romantic involvement between the sexes. Father has instructed us about that. Our primary purpose is harmony and unity. We must live it in order to teach it. Our Centers are highly moral, highly clean, and highly disciplined. Our standards must not only be as good as those of the rest of the society, but higher. Ultimate freedom lies in structure and discipline."

I liked what he was saying. I knew that success was derived from strictness and devotion. And in the fraternity I had seen what chaos had erupted at the lack of structure and discipline.

On the wall of the Center was a picture of Moon. This particular room served as Joseph's study. It was small and simple; the one window was covered by a tacked-up sheet. A pallet and an open briefcase lay on the linoleum floor. Joseph himself sat in a yoga position.

Joseph glanced at the portrait of Moon. In this picture at least, Moon seemed to be a stern, plump man with hard, intense eyes and a ruddy complexion. "We all work together to serve our True Parents," Joseph said.

His mention of True Parents made me think of my own parents.

They knew nothing of what was happening in my life. I felt guilty for not telling them, but everything had happened so fast!

"We accept their authority as ultimate," Joseph continued. "I get direct instruction from Rev. Moon. This center gets direct instruction from me. The Principle teaches that my authority must be accepted by local members as if I was Master." Once again Joseph nodded toward the portrait of Moon.

Again, I had no difficulty with these concepts. Hadn't God used special people to lead and instruct throughout history? Wasn't there in the Bible the clear teaching of a hierarchy of authority—a chain of command?

One thing had bothered me, and I decided to approach Joseph in the matter now. "Joseph," I said, "you know that I've resigned the fraternity. I want to do what's right. But we have one more week of classes in this summer session. If I could put in only several more days I wouldn't lose the hours."

Joseph smiled and answered simply, "What if Jesus' disciples had only one more week of work before they became committed to him? Do you think that Jesus would have accepted their conditional service?"

Joseph always answered questions with questions. He often used parables to illustrate his points. Frequently his points were drawn directly from Scripture.

Immediately I knew what I must do.

After the evening meal with its usual singing and good food the group grew silent and the mood changed from festive to pensive.

Joseph spoke. "Twenty-one days ago we all vowed to win a new member to the Family. Our condition to fill this promise to God ends tonight at midnight. There are only a few more hours left to fill your commitment. I want everyone who has not won a new member to leave now and try to win one between now and midnight. God will never trust us with greater blessings if we do not fulfill our promises to him."

The circle of people sat with their heads bowed in remorse over their failure. I realized that I was the only new member and that everyone except John had failed.

Joseph continued, "But we must go out with smiles and good cheer. Your faces will scare everyone away if you are sad. We must gladly fight for the kingdom."

The next few moments shocked me.

Joseph, standing in the middle of the circle, shouted at the top of his lungs, "Abojee!"

To which everyone else jumped to their feet and answered, "Mansei!"

This sequence was repeated three times. Joseph then motioned at the door and everyone ran for it, not even stopping to clean up or make plans. I sat there frozen, confused by what I had seen.

Joseph came up to me and said, "You do not have to go out. You were not part of the original condition."

"Why did John go out?" I asked.

"None of us is victorious unless all of us are. There is no joy for John if everyone else fails," Joseph answered.

It made sense. But then another question came to mind. "What was all of the shouting about?"

Joseph laughed. "You must find us a strange lot. The shouting was similar to a cheer, but done in Korean. 'Abojee' means Father and 'Mansei' means victory. It is a way we have of cheering God. He must smile on us."

I wanted to ask Joseph why he did not go out to find a new member, but I felt like that would be another one of those uncomfortable questions.

Joseph and I cleaned up the kitchen. Around midnight the rest of the Family began coming in one by one, all having failed. When they all had returned, we gathered in the empty dining room again and quietly waited for Joseph to come out of his office. Several of the members were crouched down with their faces almost on the floor. There were whispers and sobs as they prayed for forgiveness. That their commitment and promise to God meant so much made me ashamed that I had never taken my commitment quite so seriously. These people really meant it, I thought.

Since my head was bowed, I did not see Joseph come into the room. His voice startled me as he began to speak.

In a very somber tone Joseph said, "We have failed. Our Heavenly Father has had to live with the failure of his children for centuries. We are the only ones who can bring joy to his heart, and now we have failed." Joseph's eyes were red and tears welled up in them as he spoke. "He must be weeping right now." Nearly everyone in the room was crying.

"In order to pay indemnity for our failure," Joseph continued, "we must pray all night and beg his forgiveness and ask him to please trust us once more."

Joseph then asked John to set up an altar in the front room. He instructed the rest of the members to take care of whatever needed to be done and to meet again in fifteen minutes to begin their prayer vigil.

"You don't have to participate," Joseph said. "In fact, why don't you go sleep in my office? I will be praying with the members."

Several times during the night I would awaken to hear the muffled moans and sobs coming through the walls. There was even pounding on the floor. Until that point I had only experienced joy with the Family. The intensity of their sorrow matched the intensity of their joy. Deep inside it scared me.

The Unification Church is one cult that will be around for a long while, not only because of its current campaign to achieve respectability and recognition by Christian churches, but also because of its enormous financial holdings. What many people don't realize, and what I didn't realize in 1973, was that the bulk of the Unification Church's resources come from the fund raising efforts of its individual members. It has been estimated, conservatively, that those Moonies on the street corners, in shopping malls, and in supermarkets, selling candles and flowers, yield for the Church over a million dollars every five days.

The fund raising efforts by individual Moonie groups may be *said* to be a minimal part of the Church's function, but somehow it remains a very profitable one. I, too, had a part in making money for the Church.

On Friday morning Joseph was giving instructions to various members while I finished my breakfast. He had asked Debra, a new member from Utah, to do the group's laundry. He then said something about a "brother" helping her, since there was so much to do, and he looked at me.

I smiled and said, "I'd love to help."

Joseph then asked Debra to show me what needed to be done. The first thing, she said, is that we would need to go buy some detergent. I offered to drive her in my car, but she insisted that we use the Family van. As we drove over she shared her experiences of joining the Family, which were similar to mine. We laughed and even sang a song together. When we got to the store we both got out, but Debra reached in the back and grabbed a box. She shoved it in my hands.

"Here," she said. "You fund raise while I go buy what we need."

For a moment I stood absolutely still and fear spread across my face. Debra laughed.

"I don't know what to say," I protested nervously.

"Say whatever comes to your heart," she offered. Seeing my fear, Debra grabbed the box from my hand and told me to watch how she did it.

She ran up to one man getting out of his car and stood as close to him as possible as she smiled and told him about the "drug program" she was involved in. She said they were trying to keep kids off the street and were raising money by selling candles. The guy pulled out two dollars, took the candle and walked on.

Debra immediately turned and ran toward an elderly woman. Debra called out, "Good morning. Good morning." The lady, of course, turned to see who it was. Debra bounced up to her and said something about being with an "interdenominational Christian youth project" on the college campus. The woman opened her purse and handed Debra a dollar. Debra, in turn, gave her one of the smaller candles.

"See, that's not so hard," Debra said, running back toward me. "I almost have enough now to buy what I need without using any of the money Joseph gave me. Wouldn't it be wonderful to return to the center with the products we need and then to give Joseph more money than he gave us!"

I could imagine the pleasure on Joseph's face if we were to do that. So, I grabbed the box while Debra went into the store.

My first few attempts were a disaster. I was so scared that my voice would break or nothing would come out at all. I knew that I could not tell anyone that I was fund raising for the messiah or that we were building the kingdom of heaven on earth. I was most comfortable with saying that we were sponsoring a youth center and trying to improve the moral standards on campus. That wasn't a lie, but it certainly wasn't all of the truth, either.

I first approached a businessman who didn't have time to even slow down and see what I was doing. The rejection was humiliating and hard for me to deal with.

The first woman I approached seemed scared at first, but warmed up to me quickly. I think that she felt sorry for me. When she asked how much the candles cost I suddenly realized that I did not know. Seeing my confusion she reached into her wallet and handed me five dollars and told me I was a very brave young man. She walked off without even taking the candle. That was the inspiration I needed.

Debra was in the store for about fifteen minutes. By the time she returned I had made nearly $20.00. We were both very excited and couldn't wait to get back to the Center to tell Joseph. In my excitement I jumped into the van and was ready to back out when Debra stopped me.

"Before we leave we must thank our Heavenly Father for this victory. Let's pray silently." I felt so immature that I had not thought of prayer first, but was glad that we credited the success to God.

Joseph was thrilled. "You have a great future ahead of you, Chris," he said.

The rest of the members went out to witness on the campus, but Joseph requested that I stay behind. I was glad. Like fund raising, the thought of approaching people to witness to them scared me. Again, Joseph wanted me to drive him around the city while we talked and he attended to business. I told him that I wouldn't mind doing that on a permanent basis. He just smiled.

As we drove around, Joseph told me some things that really excited me. By this point I had realized that whenever they said "Father" or "Master" they were referring to Moon. When they referred to the "True Parents" they meant Moon and his wife. They reserved the term, "Heavenly Father," for God.

Joseph had been talking about the Master quite a bit. "Master has started a leadership training school at Belvedere," Joseph said. Belvedere was the first estate that the American Unification Church had purchased for Moon. It's located on the Hudson River between Irvington and Tarrytown, New York. "Master wants all of the brothers of leadership capability to go through the training," Joseph continued. "Chris, I will arrange for you to go as soon as possible."

7

Saturday
June 25, 1973
Tucson, Arizona

"Joseph," I asked, "my Mom and Dad know nothing about what has happened. What should I tell them?"

Often, before answering one of my questions, Joseph would look off into the distance and think for several minutes. At first I didn't know if he had heard me, but later I realized he was pondering his answer. Scratching his chin as he thought, he began to speak. "Parents are a tough issue. Because of their fallen natures they love you with a selfish love, not God's unconditional love. They are responsible for your sinful nature.

"Most probably they will not understand your committment," he continued after thinking a while longer. "The devil is sly and often works through those we love the most to try to get us away from God's work. At least that has been the pattern in the past."

"Well, maybe I shouldn't tell them at all," I said.

"Oh, no," Joseph responded. "That would be dishonest of us. We need to be loving, yet firm, when we deal with those that might oppose us."

"They're used to hearing from me at least once every two weeks, and I'm overdue now," I said. "I should call them soon."

"Okay," Joseph replied. "But you'll need me to coach you, so let's map out a strategy."

Joseph explained how those of old who had followed God's will against the advice of others had usually experienced great hardships and sacrifices. In fact, he said that persecution and rejection were good signs. They indicated that you were on God's side.

"And since this is the devil's world, he can offer you anything if he is trying to get you away from God. In fact," Joseph continued, "I want you to think of the material thing that you would most want if you could have anything. If that is offered to you during the next few days on the condition that you leave us, you can be sure that Satan is working on you."

More than anything, I wanted a return trip to New Zealand to see friends and renew acquaintances. Joseph advised me that the devil would use that trip to New Zealand as bait to get me to leave.

The phone rang only twice before Mother answered it.

"Hello, Mother," I said.

"Hi, Chrissie." She had a habit of calling me "Chrissie"—a holdover from my childhood. "Let me tell your Dad that you are on the phone."

I could hear Dad pick up the phone in the den. "Hi, Dad," I said. We rarely said more than hello to each other on the phone since Mother usually dominated the conversations.

Mother was full of news about my brother Ned who was in Oklahoma working on my grandparents' ranch. As usual they asked me about school and the fraternity and I tried to sound as normal as possible.

"There is something that I need to tell you," I said, interrupting Mother.

"What's that?" Mother said in her cheerful way. They were used to hearing only good news from me.

"I've decided to quit school." I paused for a moment to let them react.

"I've also decided to quit the fraternity," I added firmly. Joseph, who had been sitting beside me all this time, was signaling me to speed up the process.

"And," I told Mother and Dad, "I'm going to quit my bank job."

Joseph clenched his fist and whispered, "Be firm!"

"I'm doing this so that I can join a special organization. It's called the Unification Church."

After a few more moments of deafening silence, Mother said, "Are you sure you want to do this?"

"Yes."

"Well, if you want to do it, go ahead."

Of course, I had not asked for their permission, yet she tentatively gave it to me. In one way I sought their approval, but in another way I wanted to be a mature adult, not needing anyone's approval of my actions.

"What did you say it was called again?" Dad interjected.

"The Unification Church," I answered.

"I've never heard of it."

"Me either," Mother added. "Are you sure it's reputable?"

"You'll just have to trust me," I answered curtly.

There was a pause and then Mother said, "Why don't you come home for a few days? We haven't seen you all summer."

"Mother, I'm just too busy right now. And I have got to be prepared to go to leadership training school in New York pretty soon."

"New York?" Mother said as her voice grew faint. To someone from New Mexico, New York sounds like the end of the earth.

I heard Dad hang up the phone in the den. He was angry. Mother's voice was beginning to break as we talked.

"Now, Mother," I said, "you and Dad have always trusted me, and you'll just have to trust me now."

"But, Chris," she said.

"Listen," I interjected, "I'll call you later." At that Joseph wildly began to express his disapproval. But it was too late. Mother hung up without saying good-bye.

"Joseph," I said, putting down the receiver, "that was horrible."

"And that's why you shouldn't call them back so soon. You will just reopen the wound. You should give it time to heal and let them get used to the idea."

I stood there still somewhat shocked. Joseph walked over and put his arm around my shoulders. "Don't worry, Chris," he said. "Whether your Mom and Dad reject you or not, you have True Parents who love you with a greater love."

I had arranged to meet Travis that evening under the pretense of further trying to win him to the movement. He had called again that afternoon to encourage me to come by and visit him at work.

When I walked into the front door of the Desert Inn where he worked, I saw he was swamped with customers, so I sat down in the lobby to wait for him to finish.

A few minutes later he came over and sat down with me. "Why don't you stay around this evening and we'll go out later?" Travis suggested.

"I can't," I said, "Joseph told me to be back in an hour or so."

"What?" His voice sounded a trifle angry. "He tells you what you can and can't do? Isn't that a little juvenile?"

That was the first time Travis had questioned anything about the Family, but I could see his point. I tried to cover up. "There are some things that he needs me to do this evening," I said, "so I can't stay."

The answer didn't seem to satisfy Travis. "Are you still happy with what you're doing?" he asked me.

"Yeah, it's terrific. I just wish you understood more."

Travis slid over toward me and said, "Let me tell you something. This afternoon your mother called me. She was in hysterics. She begged me to get you out. I tried to reassure her that you were okay."

I couldn't believe what I was hearing. They were working behind my back.

Travis continued, "I felt so sorry for her. She really doesn't understand. I even cried while I talked to her. I promised that I would talk to you, but I knew that there wasn't much I could do."

Jumping to my feet, I said, "You're right, there's *nothing* that you can do. And if they call you back, tell them to call me." I headed for the door.

Travis caught me before I got outside. "Hey, don't let this come between us. Your parents love you and so do I. We just want what's best for you."

I was too angry to say anything. I just turned and walked off. Driving back to the Center seemed the only thing to do. I felt as if my parents had betrayed me by going behind my back. They robbed me of all integrity.

When I stormed into the Center, Joseph could immediately tell that something was wrong. As I unraveled what had just happened he shook his head knowingly, as if to say, "I told you so."

"It looks like Satan is going to put up a big fight for you," Joseph predicted. "You're going to suffer a lot of trials, but we'll stand behind you every step of the way." It was reassuring to know that someone would support me.

"I'm going to call Mom and Dad back right now, Joseph," I said.

"I think that's a good idea. They need to know you're in control of your life and that you can take care of yourself. Sometimes parents have a hard time letting go."

I picked up the phone to call. "Call collect," Joseph said.

"Collect? This isn't exactly something they'll want to pay for."

"But, they need to be forced into supporting you. If they really love you and want to support you they will pay for the call," Joseph explained. Strangely enough, it made sense at the time.

"Will you accept a collect call from Chris Elkins?" I could hear the operator asking.

"Yes." I heard my Mother's reply, faint and distant.

"Mother?" I asked.

"Yes."

"I just talked to Travis and I can't believe what he told me."

She began to cry. "Chrissie, I am so worried that you have gotten mixed up in something weird. You already act so different."

"Listen to me, Mother," I said sternly, "if you are concerned for me, then you deal with *me*. Not Travis. Not anyone else but me."

"Your father and I have been talking this afternoon and we feel that you have been working too hard and that we have expected far too much out of you."

She didn't know that her next line would be the one to seal me into the Unification Church.

"Why don't you come home and take a semester off and we'll send you back to New Zealand for a visit. You deserve it."

"A trip to New Zealand?" I said aloud so that Joseph could hear. He smirked and gave me that "I told you so" look again. She offered me the thing that Joseph said Satan would offer me. Satan was using the people that I loved the most.

"You just don't understand, Mother. I cannot accept that offer."

I didn't know that Dad was on the phone. He said, "You don't even sound like our son anymore. You're breaking your Mother's heart and won't even listen to reason. You're making a big mistake. And you're getting to the age that we can't undo them all anymore."

I was furious. "I don't need or want you to undo anything. It has taken you less than one day to completely turn on me. I don't know what you felt for me before, but it seems awfully cheap to me now."

"Don't do this," Mother said, crying again.

"I've got to go."

"Please don't cut us out, promise you'll call," Mother pleaded.

"I can't promise anything right now." I hung up. I turned to Joseph and suddenly my anger turned to sorrow and tears. Joseph stood there and said, "You now have a taste of the rejection that God feels every day. The tears that you shed are the same tears that he sheds over us. You've got to take this situation and promise God you'll never reject him again."

For the first time that night I prayed in the name of the True Parents.

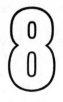

July 1973
Phoenix/Carlsbad

Days became hard to distinguish from one another. Fund raising and witnessing became the course of life. Joseph eased me into the everyday life gently, and continued to watch over me closely.

Within a few days he announced that he would travel to New York to report directly to Moon the activity and success of the Arizona team. I dreaded his absence more as the time approached. He said that he would be gone only a couple of days, but I could not imagine even a couple of days without his presence at the Center.

We had moved up to Phoenix, leaving behind a small crew to operate the Tucson Center. Joseph wanted us to go to the airport with him so we could stop at Holy Ground to pray.

When Moon had visited Phoenix several years earlier he had consecrated a small portion of a park in the center of the city and called it Holy Ground. He had blessed it by sprinkling soil from Korea on the area and then sprinkling it with Holy Salt. Holy Salt was used to rid anything of evil spirits. Whatever we brought into the Center from outside had to be sprinkled with Holy Salt. Sometimes particularly evil people were quietly sprinkled from the back without knowing it.

When we arrived at Holy Ground, we prayed in unison and Joseph gave us a little pep talk. He encouraged us to fund raise while he was gone and to expect Father to institute changes in the near future.

As we broke up to go back to the van Joseph pulled me aside. "Chris, I think that you are strong enough to go home and see your parents. You can go as soon as I get back. I'll be worrying about you, though. You know, if you ever try to leave us, I will come and get you no matter where you go."

He left me stunned. First of all, that he would let me go home, and second, that he cared so much about me that he would find me if I left. It sounded reassuring to someone who had become as dependent on him as I was.

"While I am in New York I will arrange that you and Rob go to Belvedere. Father has said that he will need new leaders. He has so many big plans. He talks about industries, political work, and other great things that we will soon be involved in. You may be needed to work in Washington someday—maybe you'll even be a senator."

I loved to hear the future talked about with such glowing expectation. The Moonies had so much hope compared to the doom that society predicted.

I was still afraid of fund raising, so I was teamed with David, a strong fund raiser.

We were assigned the parking lot in front of Goldwater's department store in Phoenix. It was a very busy area that thousands of people passed through every day. It would be a big day for us.

We were selling stale peanuts. I was told that although the peanuts were not very good, the blessing the buyer would get in heaven for having supported us made the sale justifiable.

Security guards were our biggest nemesis. On one particular day David and I were faring well, when two security guards nabbed us.

"Can't you guys read?" one guard said angrily. "We have No Soliciting signs posted all over."

David, somewhat more experienced at confronting the authorities, profusely apologized. "We're very sorry. We didn't see the signs. Our Christian young people's club is just trying to raise some money and I guess we got overzealous. We should have asked first."

This worked suprisingly well. David gave each of them a bag of our peanuts and one of the guards even suggested a couple of places where we might be able to sell our peanuts legally.

"We'll try that, sir," David said to the guard. And we turned to walk out. David was about to burst out laughing as we walked out of the parking lot. Once we were out of sight David stopped and turned around.

"Let's go back," he said.

"Are you crazy?" I responded. "They'd throw us in jail if they caught us. Especially if they ate those peanuts!"

"No," David continued, "God gave us that parking lot to work today. Satan is using those officers to keep us away. We are not going to let Satan defeat us."

I was scared to death. We crept back in and began to sell again. David said that God would bless our efforts by making our sales fruitful, and sure enough, we did well.

About an hour later a security guard rounded the corner, spotting us immediately. I signaled to David who motioned to me to follow him. We ran around the side of the building and between two cars.

"Get underneath," David ordered, and he dropped to his knees to get under a car.

"But what if—"

"Don't argue with me!" he yelled.

I got under the car. In seconds we could see the pants legs of several security guards heading our direction. In our fear it all suddenly became funny, and it was all we could do to keep from laughing out loud.

They searched for several minutes but never did find us. Once they were safely gone we crawled out from underneath and began to sell all over again. For the first time since I had begun fund raising I raised more than $150.00.

That evening we told the story to the rest of the team. With their cheers and applause we were lauded as having overcome Satan. In the middle of our revelry Joseph called.

Jill, the acting director, talked to him for several minutes. We all stood around listening and knew by her reactions and conversation that Joseph was not coming back. It was disappointing, to say the least. Joseph asked to speak to me.

"Chris," he said, "Father has given me a new mission. So, I won't be coming back." I felt like a rug had been jerked out from under me.

"I want you to go home and see your parents. As soon as you get back you will come here to New York for training. I have left instructions for Rob to come immediately." He had garnished his bad news with good news.

"And remember," he continued, "I will come get you if you don't come back from your parents. We need you."

"Thanks, Joseph," I said. "I'm going to make you proud of me."

When I pulled into Mom and Dad's drive it was almost morning. I had driven all night in order to spend as much time with them as possible. Since they both worked, I would sleep during the day while they were gone. I had stopped to see Travis in Tucson and had called them from there to let them know I was coming.

I was so apprehensive. I didn't know what to expect, and I somehow wanted everything to be normal. Yet, the next few days proved to be anything but normal.

When I walked into the house they both were still sleeping. I didn't want them seeing me so tired and bedraggled; it would only fuel their concern over my health. I crawled into my bed and fell sound asleep within minutes.

A little while later I did hear Mom and Dad open my bedroom door. I know they wanted to wake me, but I pretended to be asleep just not to have to face the emotional scene that I knew would take place.

Later that afternoon, Mother walked in the door loaded down with groceries. "I brought some stuff to make curry tonight," she said. Curry was a family tradition that we always had at special occasions. It was made from rice and a brown curry sauce and lots of assorted garnishes sprinkled on top. This, apparently, was a special occasion.

"Good," I said. "That sounds great."

"You sure look thin," she said. She had not mentioned a word about the Church, and I could tell she was trying to avoid the issue.

"I've been working hard," I said proudly. "I still weigh the same. It's just distributed."

Changing the subject, she said, "Did you mow the lawn?"

"Yeah, I knew Dad could use the break." I also knew from my

Unification Church friends that if you want to endear someone to you, then you must first serve him.

"Daddy will be pleased. He was planning to mow it this afternoon."

Except for what I took to be subtle insinuations, she never said a word about the Unification Church that afternoon. Dad arrived home a while later, pleased to see me and to see the lawn mowed. We enjoyed each other's company, but I could tell that efforts were being made not to talk about the most obvious subject.

During dinner that night the phone rang and Mother jumped up to answer it. In a minute she came back in and said, "It's long distance for you, Chris." She glanced at Dad, indicating to us all who the caller must have been, and I ran to the phone.

"Hello," I said.

"Chris?"

"Joseph!" I almost shouted.

"How's it going there?" he asked, getting to the point immediately.

"Fine, fine."

"I talked to Jill today and she said that she hadn't heard from you, so I was concerned."

"Good grief, I've only been gone twenty-four hours."

"But, you're our brother and we just want to be sure you're all right."

"Thanks," I said, "but looks like everything here is surprisingly calm."

I wasn't sure whether Mom and Dad could hear me from the dining room. I talked softly, but I noticed that I did not hear any sound coming from their direction.

"I don't need to buy an airplane ticket to come and get you?" he asked jokingly.

"I don't know," I said. "If I thought that it would get you back out here permanently I might force you to follow through on that." We both laughed.

"Call me if you need me," he said. "And be sure to call the Center every day. They want to hear from you, too."

"Okay."

We hung up and I walked back to the dining room exhilarated. But the atmosphere was so heavy when I sat down that it was startling.

"Who was that?" Mother asked.

"It was Joseph," I said. I had to bite my tongue to keep from telling her that it was none of her business.

"They want you back, don't they?" Dad asked.

"What do you mean, want me back? They knew I was going back," I answered.

That news fell like a ton of bricks.

"We thought that you had come home." Mother said tensely.

"I have come home, but just for a visit."

I began to realize that they had had other expectations. "When you called from Tucson," Mother began, "you said that you wanted to come home. We thought—"

"That I was not going back," I said, finishing her sentence. I just shook my head. "Let's don't get into this. I want to enjoy my stay with you, but I am not going to be spending the rest of my life at home." I turned and walked into the den where the TV was playing. I could hear their muffled voices in conversation in the dining room, but was not interested in what they were saying. I could envision Joseph clenching his fist and saying, "Be firm."

The next evening I prepared dinner. It was not unusual for me to cook, and I wanted to try to continue to serve Mom and Dad. We had dinner together, but little was said. I was determined not to let them depress me, so I remained as positive and cheerful as possible. I even did the dishes.

But when I walked into the den where they were sitting, I knew I was in for it.

"When are you going back?" Mother asked.

"In a couple of days."

"What are those people offering you?" Dad wanted to know.

"Dad, the Family is great. You've imagined ogres in your minds, and nothing could be further from the truth. I know that you must think that we are all sleeping together and that there's drugs and all, but it's not like that. These are really God's people."

"But, Chris," Mother said, "there are good people everywhere. You've just got to look for the good in them."

"But not like the Family. These people are *totally* sacrificial. They give all they have."

"Somehow we expected more out of you than selling flowers on the streets," Dad said.

"I won't always have to do that. But now it's our best way of raising money. Someday we'll have industries and business. For now, though, we all fund raise. This way we don't have to spend eight hours of every day making money."

After a few seconds of silence Dad spoke again, "If you had to choose between that family and this family here, which would it be?"

He was forcing me to choose sides. They had continually forced me to defend the Church, but it only made me more stubborn.

"Why would you force me to choose, Dad?" I answered, trying to avoid the issue.

"You just answered my question," he said, standing up to leave.

Mother sat there for a few minutes, searching for something to say. Without saying a word, she too got up and left. I was becoming more convinced that they were far more concerned with their own happiness than mine.

The next day, when they arrived home from work, I was packing my car. Mother said hardly two words to me and Dad didn't say a thing. They went back to their room and shut the door, mumbling things I could not understand.

I continued to pack things that I thought I might need, especially if I went to New York. I wasn't sure that they would ever want me to return.

I hesitated to tell them I was leaving, and I almost decided to leave unannounced. But I felt as if that would indicate that they had me intimidated, and I wasn't about to let that happen.

"Mother," I said, knocking at their door.

"Yes."

"I'm leaving now." It was late afternoon and I wanted to get going before it got completely dark.

There was no response from their side of the door. I just stood there for a second, expecting them to come out, but they didn't.

I turned and began to walk down the long hall toward the kitchen and out the side door to my car. Before I reached the end of the hall I heard the door open. By the time they reached me I was in the kitchen.

Mother was crying and without saying a word she grabbed at me as if I would vanish if she did not hold on. Dad had to pull her away. He was crying too.

Dad was the first to speak. "Are you sure you have to go?"

"Yes," I said, trying to be firm.

"Can we do anything to change your mind?"

75

"No," I said, tears running down my cheeks.

"Then go," he said disgustedly. Turning, he and Mother walked back down the dark hall. He stopped for a moment and in anger, turned and said, "I want you always to remember what this is doing to your mother." He turned and walked away.

The door slammed and I fought the tears all the way to my car. Once inside I felt as if I was back on my own turf. I dropped my forehead down to the steering wheel and said aloud, "No more pain, God. Please, no more pain."

On the road to Phoenix I remembered Joseph's promise about going to New York. Somehow getting as far away as possible seemed best.

August 1973
New York City

Although I had traveled the world fairly extensively, I had never been to New York. I must have looked like a country boy as I walked down the street to Grand Central Station looking up at the skyscrapers. The hustle-bustle of the city with its new sights and loud, cacophonous sounds excited me endlessly. I had no fear of the unknown and was eager to see and experience everything.

Needless to say, Grand Central was busy on a Friday afternoon around five. I carried two large suitcases and was quite clumsy in the rush of the crowds. Inside the station I was amazed at the architecture and the immensity of the building. And as I stared up at the large clock that could be seen from all over, I was surprised to hear someone speaking to me.

"Hello, my name is Susan," she said to me. She was young and attractive and she radiated a purity and confidence that I found intriguing.

She went on, "I'm working with a local Christian group and we are selling tickets to hear the Korean evangelist Rev. Moon speak at Carnegie Hall." Her smile never left her face as she spoke.

Excitedly, I interrupted her before she had a chance to finish. "Me, too," I said. "I am one of you!"

She looked at me curiously, tilting her head a little. "You're in the Family?"

"Yes," I said. "I'm from the Arizona Family. I'm here to sing in the choir."

"Oh, it's so good to see a new brother!" she said. Susan turned and shouted to another girl down the way, "Karen, here is a brother who will be in the choir."

Karen waved and smiled, but continued to sell tickets. She wasn't having much success.

"How are the ticket sales going?" I asked.

"Not well. Satan is very strong in New York. We are having to fight him every day. Say, do you know which train to take to Belvedere?"

"No. This is my first time here."

"Well, follow me," Susan said. "I'll show you."

Susan led me to the ticket booth and then to the Belvedere train. She spoke glowingly of all of the brothers and sisters arriving in New York for the program at Carnegie Hall. She said that she envied my position in the choir, but was glad that she was on the "front lines" fighting Satan.

The citizens of New York had become used to the street evangelism of the Moonies. Moon's picture could be seen on large posters placed on every street in the city. At construction sites the fences were covered with the posters heralding Moon's appearance at Carnegie Hall. But for someone as far away from the center of activity as I was, the widespread impact of all this publicity was a surprise. I was just now beginning to realize the remarkable potential that the movement had.

I had never been on a train before. Looking around, I saw advertising above the doors and windows. To my astonishment, above the door across from me was a picture of Moon. Even here the name of Moon was being promoted. Up till now I had seen few pictures of Moon, and I found this one strange and ominous. His short-cropped Korean hair was combed straight back. His face was neutral, showing almost no expression except for a faint smile. The picture was in blue tones, rather than black and white. Immediately beside his picture ran the caption, "Christianity in Crisis."

Seeing the poster stunned me. After meeting Susan and Karen, I was reeling with excitement. I had been used to the Family being a small, nearly insignificant group in Arizona. Here, in New York, it seemed a powerful force.

After months of being told about Belvedere and after weeks of waiting to see it in person, my expectations were high. Even so, my anticipations weren't substantial enough to conceive of a place as grand as Belvedere actually was. When I finally saw the walled estate, my mouth dropped open. Everything that Joseph had told me about Belvedere was exactly true.

At first, you couldn't see it. It was set far back behind a four-foot stone wall, sculptured lawns, and gently rolling hills dotted with trees. The estate overlooked the Hudson.

The house itself was situated on a little knoll at the end of the drive. It was more of a mansion than a house, sizable but not huge, with a sandstone front and carved, walnut-stained double doors. It was not ornate, yet well-to-do, and it seemed to be thirty or forty years old. I was let off at the front door.

I had visions of being greeted warmly by a dozen or so Family members inside. But the place seemed quiet. I wasn't sure whether to knock or to walk in. I decided to walk in, but just as I put my hand to the doorknob someone behind me shouted.

"Hey, you."

I turned to see a man in his thirties running toward me. He had prematurely lost some of his hair, but otherwise seemed quite young. "Who are you?" he shouted at me.

"Chris Elkins. From the Arizona Family. I'm here to join the choir."

"Why are you going in there?"

"Isn't this Belvedere?" I asked.

"Sure," he said. "But you aren't staying in there. Only the True Parents stay in there." He stopped a few paces from me and smiled. "Hi, I'm Bobby," he said.

"Hello."

"You'll be staying down there." Bobby pointed across the lawn at what appeared to be remodeled stables.

I saw now that the mansion wasn't the only building on the grounds. Not only were there the "stables" but also a cottage and some other buildings.

I now realized my mistake — the presumption of walking into the home of Moon himself! But I was too excited to be embarrassed. On the walk down to the other buildings, Bobby told me that most of the others were out in the city selling tickets. But the choir members would be back early to practice. Bobby took me into the "stables." We walked up a wooden staircase into a large, dimly lit area. Naked light bulbs dangled from the ceilings and cast a glaring, shadowed light. There was a shower running and someone singing. Bobby took me into Room F—the size of two average bedrooms. It held at least twenty bunk beds. The room overflowed with suitcases, clothes, shoes, and toiletries all scattered around.

"Find an unmade bed and claim it," Bobby said.

Later, after Bobby left, I felt miserably alone. For the first time, I realized that at Belvedere I would no longer be one of twenty as I had been in Arizona, but now I would be one of hundreds. I felt insignificant and no longer special. It worried me that here I would be a stranger and I wouldn't know anyone. This was one of my first disillusionments about the Church. Though I had brought it upon myself, I now understood that the Family wasn't quite as "intimate" as it had first appeared to be, and that the Church had larger purposes.

Later, I was still in awe over the estate. The sun had set, and the moon shone brightly as I made my way across the grounds to the cottage where the choir was to meet. The big house seemed to shimmer in the moonlight. Although it wasn't cold there was a chill in the air; at least, it *seemed* chilly compared to the balmy Arizona nights I was used to. The greenery struck me, as well. Little in Arizona is green, so the lawns, trees, and shrubs of Belvedere seemed especially beautiful.

There was a light on in the big house, and I wondered as I walked by if Moon was in there. I was curious to see him, but after talking with Bobby I knew better than to assume I was welcome there. I continued on toward the cottage.

I understood why it was called an artist's cottage. It looked much like an oversized cabin and was nestled in a particularly lush part of the estate. It was virtually cut off from the rest of the facilities and you felt alone there. The steep, wood-shingled roof was reminiscent of Swiss architecture and was accented by tall windows and wood siding. I could see activity inside as I approached the door.

But this time, instead of walking right in, I decided to knock. A voice that bade me to enter not only conveyed the message, but did it musically. I opened the door to see a few people sitting near a fireplace, reviewing the sheet music they held in their hands.

"And who are you?" the same musical voice asked. I told them who I was and where I had come from. "Good," the voice answered. "We have been expecting you." I saw now who it was that was speaking, or singing, to me. He was young and very animated, and he stood with a young woman who wore no makeup. "I am Randy and this is my wife Linda," he said. "We conduct the choir." Although it did not clearly register with me at the time, they were the first married couple I had met in the movement.

"What part do you sing?" Randy asked.

Before I could answer, Linda interrupted, "Can't you see that Chris is cold? Let him warm up before you quiz him." Linda showed me where there was coffee and tea, and she told me to help myself.

The atmosphere in the cottage was cozy. Linda played the piano while others attempted to learn their parts. A fire crackled in the fireplace. I sat and listened until I felt sufficiently warm and relaxed to get involved.

Within an hour all of the choir members arrived. At first I felt like an outsider, but before long I joined in the conversation and was having a good time. The choir members spoke of the difficulty of selling tickets in New York. Although the prospect of street work in the big city scared me, it was also intriguing, and I began to look forward to the experience.

We had just begun our practice when a short Oriental man walked into the cottage. He was middle-aged and fairly small. We were in the middle of a song when he came in, but suddenly everyone quit singing and began to whisper. I knew that it wasn't Moon; the name that I kept hearing whispered was Mr. Kim.

"Father is very excited about choir," he said in his Oriental English. "He want to see you this night."

The whispering and excitement grew suddenly intense. Moon wanted to see us! Mr. Kim made arrangements with Randy for us to be at the main house in thirty minutes. As he left, Mr. Kim turned and said, "Mansei for True Parents!" to which everyone repeated "mansei."

Randy had to shout at us to bring us back to order. Several of the girls were teary eyed, and suddenly the atmosphere was electric.

"That Father wants to see us means that he thinks that we are

81

very special. Let's practice a couple of songs that we all know because I am sure that he will want to hear us sing," Randy instructed.

The consensus was to sing "Shining Fatherland," which I had never heard before. It had a pleasant melody with a descant part that the girls sang. I just had to fake it. The excitement of seeing Moon overrode any element of fear.

While walking up to the main house I spoke with a couple of the choir members, Kevin and Jim, who were from the New Hampshire family.

"Have you ever seen Father before?" Jim asked Kevin and me.

"No," I said, "I've only been in the Family two months. This is my first time at Belvedere."

Kevin answered next. He looked a lot like the actor Paul Newman. Although his face was a little thin, he looked as if he was in his teens. "Yes, I have seen and heard him many times," was Kevin's reply.

Jim then answered his own question as we got into view of the main house. "This is my first time, too," he said. "I am so excited. Can you imagine meeting the messiah?"

Kevin added, "Many saints of old have died so that this day might come. We are truly a privileged people."

Although Kevin looked young, his comments reflected a maturity beyond his years.

"How long have you been in the Family?" I asked him.

"Five years."

"Five years!" I almost shouted. "How old are you, anyway?"

"Nineteen."

"That means you joined when you were fourteen?"

He nodded. I looked at Jim. He was just as stunned as I was. Jim's question was exactly what came to my mind first. "What did your parents think?"

"Well," Kevin replied, as if he had told the story a hundred times, "my mom and sister and I were living in Italy after my parents divorced. Mom started going to the lectures the Family was giving in Rome and got me to go along with her. In the end she did not join, but I did. My father, who lived in California, got upset and came and got me and took me back to Berkeley where he was living. What he did not realize was that there was a Center right down the street from him that I went to every day after school.

After a while he got tired of keeping up with me and let me move into the Berkeley Family."

"Amazing," was all I could say.

Then Jim said, "My parents fight me every day about this. I can't believe that your parents let you move in when you were only fourteen." I shook my head in agreement.

By this time we were almost to the main house. Randy, who was walking several yards ahead, stopped in order to gather us all together before we entered. He said a short prayer and we went inside.

The foyer in the main house was big enough for sixty of us to comfortably stand in. Although the house was not elaborate inside, it was tastefully elegant. I was told that Moon himself had directed the interior design.

Mr. Kim met us once again and explained how Moon wanted us to meet him. We were to file into the dining room one by one, bow, then stand there until he motioned for us to take our place in the choir formation. The women were to enter first.

Everyone quickly combed his hair and brushed off his clothes in order to look as nice as possible. Several girls held hands. We all were brimming with anticipation.

The girls entered the dining room. The line moved quickly, and with each step forward my heart beat faster. By the time I was next in line, I was on the verge of cardiac arrest. What would he be like? What would he say? Will he like me? Dozens of questions, feelings, and fears whizzed through me in a matter of seconds.

When it was my turn to enter, I almost froze. Mr. Kim motioned for me to move quickly. Inside the dining room stood a large oak dining table, which would seat nearly twenty. Several people sat at the other end of the table, but only one sat at the head.

Moon!

10

August 1973
Belvedere/New York City

Rather plump, with his arms folded, Moon carried the same expression that the picture in the train had displayed. As I bowed I was almost afraid to take my eyes off him. Once I straightened back up again, I just stood there waiting for his signal to move. For several seconds, which seemed like hours, he stared at me. I had been told that he could see your spiritual makeup just by looking at you. One's sins and shortcomings were always on display in his eyes. He didn't make a sound. And then, with a motion so slight that unless you were closely attentive you would not have caught it, he signaled for me to join the others at the far end of the room. Once again, Mr. Kim snapped at me to move on.

All the other choir members stood at attention, in choir formation, and smiled a less-than-natural grin. It seemed odd to me, but then I followed suit. Randy and Linda were the last to enter. Moon said something in Korean to Randy which Mr. Kim quickly translated. Moon had asked us to sing.

Our selection of "Shining Fatherland" greatly pleased him. He smiled and spoke to some of the others sitting at the table with him. All who sat at the table were Orientals—some Japanese and some Korean.

Moon wanted to hear the same song over and over. After a bit, I began to catch on to the words. It was a good thing, too. At one point Moon stood in front of each choir member and listened carefully. He wanted to hear each voice singing. Naturally, I was scared to death. But when Moon stood in front of me, it happened to be a section of the song that I knew, and I made no mistakes.

Later Moon told us that we would be responsible for preparing the hearts of the audiences to which he would speak. If we won their sympathies with our singing, then they would more readily accept his words. He said that we would be the John the Baptist that would prepare the way for him.

We were in that room for more than an hour. Every so often Moon would be interrupted by someone bringing him a message or asking him a question. Once an Oriental man brought what must have been bad news. Immediately Moon flew into a rage, yelling and shouting at the man who had been the bearer of the news. The poor Oriental man backed up and bowed again and again as he edged out of the room. Moon said something to Mr. Kim, who then jumped up and left. And then, Moon turned to us and was suddenly back in a pleasant mood.

My first impressions of Moon were etched in fear. Everyone felt intimidated by him. Although he smiled occasionally, we never really relaxed or felt at our ease. When we were dismissed it was a relief.

But we were to see more of Moon. At 5:00 A.M. someone marched into our sleeping room, switched on the lights, and announced that Moon would speak in forty-five minutes and that everyone was to be ready.

The scramble out of bed was remarkable. The noise was excruciating, with all the shouting and cheering. I was less than excited about getting up that early but there was no way I could stay in bed. There was no time to take a shower. Besides, the plumbing was bad. As we filed out, Kevin told me of Moon's speaking habits.

"Father often likes to speak early in the morning," he said. "He sleeps less than any of us do and we have no right to complain of little sleep. Since what he says has to be translated, his talks take twice as long as if they were spoken in English. It is not unusual for him to speak for six hours." My body started to ache just thinking about it.

When we got to the room, everyone was crowding in. We all

had to sit on the floor, which added to the discomfort. We were packed in so tightly that we couldn't move.

A half hour later Moon arrrived. Mr. Kim had already started us singing and praying. Since there were close to 300 of us, the din from the many vocal prayers was deafening. The prayers were not just prayers of thanksgiving, but prayers of pain and sobbing and prayers claiming victory after hard fighting. The principle seemed to be that God would hear the loudest prayer.

Moon entered with his wife. Mrs. Moon, Hak Ja Han, was stunningly beautiful. Yet she had borne seven children for Moon since their marriage in 1960. Mrs. Moon rarely, if ever, spoke publicly, but she was always present where Moon was.

This morning Moon was upset about the dismal ticket sales. He asked everyone to stand who had not sold a single ticket. By this time I thought that Moon would be able to tell just by looking at me that I had not done any ticket selling. But technically, I had not sold any. I stood up and Moon promptly called on me to explain why I hadn't sold any tickets.

"I only arrived last night," I said.

Everyone laughed, and so did Moon. He said that my excuse was a good one. But others were not so lucky. For those who had not sold tickets, Moon was merciless. His attacks were scathing. He said that we were lazy and uncaring. He said that we weren't helping build the kingdom of heaven on earth.

There was something here that disturbed me, although it was something I wasn't conscious of until years later. These, Moon's disciples, had *tried* to sell tickets—they had just not been successful. I learned how important *results* were to Moon and to the Unification Church. Here, results took precedence over methods. It didn't matter what each Moonie's attitude had been, or what efforts had been expended. It mattered only that there was nothing to show for it.

Not only did I, too, have to sell tickets—I was chosen to be a co-captain. A Japanese, Hashie, was the leader. He told us, before we went out that morning, that we should be willing to give our very lives in order to sell tickets. He said, too, that his ability as a team leader would be judged by the total number of tickets sold.

We were dropped off in pairs on various street corners in

Manhattan. Our area was near Times Square; it was a hot-bed of activity. Hashie paired off the members and let them off with a map. Everyone would be picked up at 7:00 P.M. No one had any money, but each person was given a paper bag with a sandwich and a piece of fruit in it. Hashie gave us fifty cents for something to drink.

Because I was co-captain, I was teamed with Hashie. He was truly remarkable. Though he didn't speak English very well, he could stop a businessman on the street and sell him a $3.00 ticket easily. I, on the other hand, couldn't get anyone to even listen to me. They'd keep on walking by as if they didn't hear. It was humiliating.

Hashie taught me how to step in front of someone to get their attention. He told me to shout, "Look out!" or "Help!" just to get people to listen. Several New Yorkers were already disgruntled with Moon's style of sales, however. Often I was shoved, yelled at, even spit upon by people who were tired of being accosted on every street corner.

Within several hours I had sold two tickets; Hashie had sold seven. I asked him how he managed to do so well.

"I pray to True Parents to sell ticket for me," he said. "People say to me, 'I don't know why I buy ticket from you.' But I know. True Parents are always with us."

That day our team had sold fifteen tickets. Hashie had sold nine of them. Hashie was disappointed. He told us how he'd have to crawl to Moon since his team's results were so bad.

In the evenings we would rehearse the music for the big Carnegie Hall program. We would sleep only four hours a night in order to have time to sell tickets and rehearse as well. Hashie was given another assignment, and I was made team leader. It was a position that I didn't really deserve, yet I was glad to have it. Being team leader won me respect in Randy and Linda's eyes and allowed me once again, even in the midst of 300 Moonies, the feeling of being special.

I saw Joseph about a week after I arrived at Belvedere. We had all met in Central Park at a place the movement had dubbed "Holy Ground." Every state had a Holy Ground that had been blessed by Moon. Often the members met there to pray. Moon had sprinkled salt—"Holy Salt"—and Korean soil in those areas to sanctify them.

There were about a thousand of us in Central Park that crisp New York morning. Carnegie Hall was almost upon us and Moon was speaking to us now every day.

As I ran to the top of the hill to join the crowd I saw Joseph. I was so excited to see him that I grabbed him and held him like a long-lost brother. He responded but put his hand over my mouth. Moon was speaking and the clamor I was creating had been distractive. It was hard for me to restrain my enthusiasm, but I felt good and secure just standing next to Joseph.

After Moon spoke, Joseph had little time to talk. I told him that I had been made a team leader, and the smile that spread across his face was worth a million words. Joseph, however, didn't have time to chat; he was an important leader in New York then, and he had major commitments.

That evening at the dining hall I sat alone to eat. From where I sat I could look out a door and see the big house shimmering in the evening light. There were streams of people going to and from Father's Rock behind Moon's house. Father's Rock was a popular place for prayer—Moon himself was often there. It was a large boulder that jutted up into the air at an angle, and which overlooked the Hudson. It was not unheard of for Moonies to be there in the driving rain or even to stay there and pray all night. I went there once a day, oftentimes with one of my new-found brothers from the choir.

Just then, I felt a hand on my shoulder. It was Randy. "Are you busy?" he asked me. "Mr. Salonen needs someone to drive him to Boston tonight, and I thought you might wish to help."

Although I was very tired, I jumped at the opportunity. Neil Salonen was president of the Unification Church. He was an outstanding leader and speaker. I had admired him from a distance, but had never met him. He wielded more influence with Moon than any other American.

"You're not too sleepy, are you?" Randy asked.

"No!" I said emphatically. "When do we leave?"

"In an hour. You're to meet him in the kitchen of the main house."

By this time I considered the main house to be the kingdom of heaven. Just to go in it, or even be near it seemed like a special privilege. Excitedly, I ran to my room and changed clothes—I wanted to look my best.

When I arrived at the kitchen of the main house I met Salonen's personal assistant, Marc Lee. Marc always looked exhausted. He had to keep pace with Salonen, who had to keep pace with Moon.

Marc was too tired to drive that night, and that's why I got the chance to drive. Salonen would be delayed till 2:00 A.M. We would sleep for a few hours in a small room off of the kitchen until he arrived.

I was too excited to sleep, however. Marc dropped off almost immediately, and left me awake, thinking. So much was happening so quickly. I hadn't had time to sort everything out. Sure, there were some things that had troubled me about the Church, such as its size and Moon's demeanor, but there were positive things too—the love of so many wonderful people and the urgent sense of mission. This was Christianity in *action*.

When we finally drove off that night, Marc and I sat in front while Salonen stretched out in back. We had talked for some time when Salonen suddenly sat up and asked where I was going.

"To Boston, I think."

"You're going in the opposite direction," Salonen said disgustedly. "Why didn't you direct him, Marc?"

"I'm sorry, Mr. Salonen," Marc answered.

"This is the most important car in America on the road tonight," Salonen said. "Satan will try to delay us, or throw us off. Marc, you stay awake with Chris so that this does not happen again."

Salonen lay back down again and Marc sat up attentively. We turned around and headed in the right direction.

The drive was long, and Marc soon fell asleep. I was awfully sleepy, as well, but kept biting my tongue or pinching my leg in order to stay awake. About an hour outside of Boston, Salonen sat up in the back seat. He saw that Marc had fallen asleep, and I was afraid that he would lash out at Marc. Instead, though, he took compassion and smiled.

"He's awfully tired," Mr. Salonen said.

"Yeah," I said, "but he did do a good job of keeping me awake while he lasted." I still wasn't sure that Salonen wouldn't be angry.

"Marc is a good man," Salonen said. "He takes every step that I take and never complains. He has a big heart, too, and often helps me temper my decisions with a more loving point of view. He's good to have around."

I hung on to every word that he was saying. It was still dark outside so we could see little of the countryside.

"Tell me a little bit about yourself," Salonen commented.

"Well," I said, "there isn't a whole lot to tell. I joined the Family about ten weeks ago in Arizona. I was a college senior, a fraternity president when I met Joseph Shepard and the One World Crusade in Tucson. I joined in a week and had been there until being called up for the choir."

Salonen seemed to be listening to everything attentively. I was really impressed with him.

"What about your family?" he asked.

"I'm afraid that they haven't been too receptive to the idea. I think they'll come around, though. They had such high ideals for me. I think they thought that I might be in politics some day."

Salonen sat up a little bit when I mentioned politics. "Were you involved in politics?" he asked.

"Yes," I said, "primarily in Republican politics. I was quite active in Young Republicans at college."

"You know about our Freedom Leadership Foundation in Washington, don't you?" Salonen asked.

"I heard a little about it from the Arizona Family, and I saw one of their newspapers, *The Rising Tide*," I answered.

"I'm always looking for prospective staff people."

This was exciting! There was nothing that I loved more than politics, and I'd jump at the opportunity to be in Washington. But I knew better than to *ask* for the position. One was awarded those kinds of positions.

"You would probably make a good staff person there. Have you had any journalism?" Salonen further inquired.

I couldn't believe how well this was working out. "Yes," I said, perhaps too eagerly, "I was the feature editor on my high school newspaper and did some writing in college."

Salonen seemed impressed. "I'll have to keep you in mind," he said. "We'll see what we can do."

11

October 1973
Carnegie Hall/The National Tour

The program at Carnegie Hall represented the climax of weeks of preparation. The city had been overwhelmed by people the press now called "Moonies." Our notoriety was a key to our success. Had the press ignored us, we would have failed miserably.

The choir had practiced hours on end. During the last few days of September we didn't go into the city at all, but practiced day and night. We were exhausted, and there was a great deal of tension. It wasn't unusual for tempers to flare. This, too, was a disillusionment. After all, the life of the Moonies that I had known was one of ideal love and perfection. But apparently that couldn't last. And when placed under such crushing pressures, we all fell a little apart.

Standing on stage at Carnegie Hall was one of the most memorable experiences of my life. It was exhilarating to know that within moments the curtain would open and we would perform in one of the most prestigious showplaces in America. And we all knew that the audience's first impression of Moon would come from the choir. It was important for us to do well.

Randy, trying to keep us calm, was a nervous wreck. Right before the curtains parted he winked at me, but I could tell from his strange smile that he was tense.

The curtains opened. A mellow voice announced, "Ladies and

Gentlemen, the New Hope Singers International." The lights were bright, but in a second I realized that the hall was less than half full. We all were noticeably shaken, and only Randy was able to keep us emotionally stable.

We had been told that enough tickets had been sold that people would have to be turned away in droves. Yet, the turnout had been dismal. I noticed, though, as we were singing that the hall began to fill up. By the time that we were finished almost every seat had been filled. I, as well as the others, noticed that it was Family members filling up the seats before Moon appeared on the stage. When Moon walked out, the house was full!

After we finished, we went up into the balcony and listened to Moon speak. He was speaking in Korean and would pause occasionally to let a man named Bo Hi Pak translate for him. I expected Moon to be gentle and compassionate with his audience, but he presented a tirade of vocal scoldings as his arms were flung in every direction.

In less than thirty minutes large numbers of people were getting up and walking out. I could hardly blame them, too. Moon was tedious to listen to, and insulting to his listeners. He showed no compassion, only judgmental temper. He was jeered from the audience several times, but continued. It was as if a battle had started.

I sat in the balcony in shock. I could not believe what I was witnessing. Moon was giving no one a chance to accept him. With every person that got up and walked out, I became increasingly saddened.

Back at Belvedere that night I went immediately to Father's Rock and cried. Had it been worth it all? Moon was going to speak two more nights in Carnegie Hall and I didn't know if I could take it. And to think that I had to witness that scene in twenty more cities across the nation!

Kevin came up and joined me at the rock. He, too, had been crying, but I knew that he would work on cheering me up. There was a slight drizzle falling, and it was cold. But we stood there and voiced prayers asking for strength and understanding. Kevin said that he had something for me and we walked back toward the living quarters. I was so depressed that I nearly left immediately to go back to Arizona or even back home.

We walked down into a rather musty basement where Kevin flicked on a light. We were totally alone and he seemed to know his way around.

"You've been here before, haven't you?" I asked.

"Yeah," Kevin said. "There is a special gift that I want to share with you. One of my favorite brothers shared it with me once when I was depressed and it cheered me up."

Kevin then carefully reached into his front pocket and pulled out a white handkerchief and began to unfold it.

"Come over here," he said, bidding me to look closer at his surprise.

When he finished unwrapping it, there in the middle of his hand was a chunk of something that looked almost like a pebble. Kevin's face was lit with excitement as he brought the item closer to my face.

"Do you know what it is?" he asked.

"No, I don't think so," I said, bewildered.

"Well, you know that the most important event in all of history was when Father married Mother. That was the marriage feast of the lamb referred to in Revelation. Well, this is a piece of the cake that was served at that wedding." In other words, what I was looking at was a thirteen-year-old piece of cake.

Kevin took a knife, cut it in half, and gave half to me. Kevin's awe over the cake was fascinating. He was like a little child with a new toy. I thanked him profusely for it and promised him I would treasure it. He asked me to share half of my portion with someone else some day.

As we were leaving, Kevin said, "You know that Father has been married more than once, don't you?"

My jaw practically dropped to the floor. "No," I said. "I hadn't heard that." The news really disturbed me. "Then, if Father is the messiah," I asked, "why didn't he marry the right woman the first time?"

Kevin's answer was well thought out. Obviously someone had told him how to answer the question. "God had prepared several women to fill the role of being the new Eve. But, since they would all have to be raised out of imperfection to perfection by Father, there was a possibility that the woman could fail. After all, it was Eve who first failed in the beginning. Well, Father's first wife failed. His mission could not be held back because of her, so God prepared our Mother for him."

"Will she fail?" I asked.

"Their marriage will be considered at the perfection stage after she bears twelve children for Father, and is married to him for twenty-one years. In 1981 the True Parents will be at perfection stage."

A lot of that was news to me. I later learned that Moon had not only been married once before, but at least twice before, with some claiming that he had been married as many as five times.

Life at Belvedere was comfortable compared to what we experienced over the next few months on tour. More than once we did not have enough money to stay in a motel and had to sleep in the vans. The gasoline crisis affected our tour and often we would be stranded for several hours, shivering and freezing in the cold.

There was never any excuse for not selling tickets. The rougher the weather, the more determined we were supposed to be. We never went hungry, but often we had only stale sandwiches to eat.

Moon never changed his style of speaking. The rejection that he received was pretty widespread across the country.

The tour ended in Los Angeles. While there I was selected for an important task. The local Unification Church had set their eye on Pat Boone to attend one of our functions, and thus give it credibility in the eyes of a lot of Christians. We discovered where Boone went to church and began attending with him on Sunday mornings.

He was a very kind and gracious man. I believe that from the beginning he knew who we were, but never once did he say a harsh word to us or try to reject us. We were encouraging him about attending a banquet we were having. If we could get him to sit at the head table many people would consider us a lot more credible, simply by his presence. He wouldn't even have to say anything. His presence would be enough for us.

At church over several Sundays we could never get him to commit himself to attend our function. We began giving him some of our literature, hoping that he would respond to us. Interestingly enough, he returned our literature to us the following Sunday. In it he had marked where he believed that we had misquoted the Bible or had lifted it out of context. Often, in the margins he would write, "I don't believe this" or, "This isn't true." Even though he challenged our beliefs, he never once was harsh to us. He loved us, and yet at the same time showed us that we were wrong. For many of us he planted a seed in our minds that matured as time went on. He knew the key to our most vulnerable points: biblical fidelity and unconditional love.

During this time I had phoned my parents every two or three

weeks. Their criticism of me had waned a bit. We enjoyed hearing each other's voices. Though they still didn't approve of what I had done, and though they were quite bitter toward the Unification Church itself, we managed to get along all right long distance.

Once when the national tour swung through Dallas, I asked my parents if they would agree to come and hear Moon speak. They did indeed come to hear Moon and the event was something of a disaster. They were more convinced than ever that I had made a terribly wrong decision in my life.

En route to Washington, D.C., from Los Angeles, where the tour had ended, the choir happened to stop in Carlsbad where my parents lived. Randy asked me to call them and see if they'd be willing to fix a breakfast for us. I didn't want to, but Randy was firm. Surprisingly, my parents agreed to it.

And so, at six-thirty one morning we rolled into my parents' driveway in Carlsbad. They had prepared enough breakfast for sixty people and allowed us to use their three bathrooms to clean up. I was particularly impressed with my parents. Although they still disagreed with me and everything that I was doing, they never failed to love me at every opportunity they had. (In the end, I realized it was my parents that had the unconditional love for me, not the Family. The Family's love was often more tangible, but Mom and Dad's love was more durable and far more unconditional. They loved me even when I went against their wishes. The Family, I later learned, loved me only when I was doing what they wanted me to do.)

We left Carlsbad and kept heading east on our four-day journey to Washington, D.C. We would stop along the way and "blitz" towns. All sixty of us would be dropped off in a rather small town and for a few hours, usually less than three, we sold candy to every person in sight. It was not unusual for us to make $1000 per blitz. We always remained financially solvent, owed in great part to people's willingness to accept us at face value. We looked good and told them we were doing good things. We never really told lies, but rarely told all of the truth, either.

Often we would fake accents to make our international name more real. Randy was great at an Irish accent and could charm people in an instant into buying a box of Cracker Jacks for a dollar.

Once we arrived in Washington, things began to change rapidly for me. On the first evening we were there, I heard Mr. Salonen mention my name to some people from the Freedom Leadership

Foundation. Then Randy came up and said he had something he wanted to talk to me about.

"Chris," he said, "you have really proven yourself as willing to accept God's will for your life these last few weeks. I really worried about you for a while. But, I have the confidence that you could be an excellent leader someday."

"Thanks," I said. "It's good to know that my efforts have not gone unnoticed."

"Well," Randy began, "I am not the only one who has noticed. Mr. Salonen has, too."

I was getting excited. I felt I knew what Randy was getting ready to say.

"Mr. Salonen," Randy continued, "wants you to go to the Freedom Leadership Foundation. I know you may be excited about the possibility, but it is awfully hard work and requires being totally faithful to the True Parents. You don't get much of a chance to deepen spiritually there. I just hope that you have deepened enough to hold your own."

"Randy," I said, "this is what I have been praying for. I need to do something that will be a challenge to me, something that I am good at. Ever since I've been in the Family I have wanted to be here in Washington."

"If this is what you really want, then I don't want to stand in your way. I want you to know, though, that you have been one of my favorite persons in the choir, and I would love to keep you."

We shared a few minutes of silence. I remembered the time we had been in New Orleans and had no place to stay. The Church had forgotten to make arrangements for the choir, so for three days and nights we lived in vans.

Every Sunday morning at five, the Family everywhere rises to say a pledge to the True Parents. The men group to one side of the room, and the women to the other. Everyone bows to a picture of the True Parents three times and reads a pledge. The essence of the pledge is that one acknowledges Moon and his wife as the True Parents and would be willing to do anything necessary to bring about their will on earth.

This particular Sunday morning in New Orleans, since we were living in vans and had nowhere to go, we had to say the pledge outside in the street. This area was slightly run-down and police drove by periodically. Randy insisted that we say the pledge. But it wouldn't be right to attract attention. Randy decided that the least ostentatious thing to do would be to say the pledge while walking.

And so we did. It was chilly that morning and the gulf air was heavy and wet. We walked along and said the pledge. Still, I am sure that sixty people walking down the streets of New Orleans at five in the morning and mumbling a chant is less than discreet. But with Randy that was the way things were done.

"Will you be going in the morning, Chris?" Randy was asking me.

"That'll be fine," I said. "Thanks again."

Randy reached over and patted me on the back; then he turned and left. I was so excited about my new assignment that I could hardly hold still. I told several of the brothers in the choir and they all seemed to be genuinely happy for me. Kevin was especially happy. We had become good friends during the tour, and I knew that he, too, wanted to do something else besides choir. His problem was that he was too young, even though he had been in the Family nearly six years.

12

January—August 1974
Washington D.C.

At first it was our aim in the Unification Church to secure publicity at any cost—even if such media attention focused on bad news. Notoriety, it was reasoned, was better than nothing. Public ignorance was the worst thing that could happen to the movement. Consequently, there were the Moon crusades, the national tours, and random, desperate attempts to step into the public eye. Even if vast numbers were not flocking to the Church, the name of Moon was becoming a buzz word in the news.

But later, it was thought that perhaps *influence* was more important, or at least that the mad grab for power, especially as it occurred in Washington, would lead to great amounts of publicity—a fame that would cast the movement favorably with the American people. This was where I came in.

The Unification Church began to infiltrate the nation's capital. It was all legal, of course—or mostly. Lobbying by special interests is the standard in Washington. But, then, the ways we went about it were particularly clever, sometimes sneaky.

One of the ways in which the Unification Church wedged itself into good political position was by supporting reelection campaigns. Senators with a conservative and anti-Communist bent were usually the targets of the Family's strategy. (The Unification Church, of course, has traditionally maintained a conservative profile and has long opposed Communism—a political view that aligns many Moonies with many evangelical Christians. Often, they have worked side-by-side, supporting the same causes.)

The organized support of political campaigns by nonprofit groups is illegal, but no one can stop an individual from volunteering his or her services. This was how the Unification Church worked it. Several "individuals" would volunteer to serve: "Senator Smith, I like your positions on defense and the decaying state of national morality. You're the person I'd like to see elected. I have sixty hours a week free and I've had extensive experience in fund raising and public relations. May I help you with your campaign?" Not only would a Senator jump at such a volunteer, but more than likely that volunteer would be a prize catch and treated as such. And when these volunteers arrived at campaign headquarters at five or six every morning, seven days a week, hours before another soul showed up, and then left late into the night, hours later than anyone else went home, they would more often than not shoot to the top of the organization. Later, they'd be in position to receive key favors when the candidate won the election.

At one time there were more than 200 Moonies working in Washington. I was one of them.

It had been eight months since I had joined the Church. But in Washington you didn't think much about the past. What mattered was what happened. Events, votes, bills—that's what counted.

While in Washington I hadn't had much time to think about myself. As a member of the Freedom Leadership Foundation, and editor of its newspaper, *The Rising Tide*, I was thoroughly preoccupied with the task of nosing out the news in Congressional corners and also with distributing our paper to key people. But my role was changing.

Over lunch I spoke with Mitsuko, an Oriental who was a member of the National Prayer and Fast Committee.

"We want you to help us with Nixon's support," she said.

"You seem to be doing quite well."

She smiled. "Yes, I suppose we are."

"His support seems to be holding up."

Mitsuko nodded. "But these things change quick. Overnight, sometimes. We have to persevere. We want your help again, Chris."

"Okay," I said.

"First, thanks for helping with Father's Watergate Statement."

"It served the movement."

"We got especially good exposure. Newspapers all over ran it."

"What else is up?" I asked.

Mitsuko leaned over to me and said. "We need to win Nixon's favor. You know how much he can help us."

"Sure."

"We're organizing rallies in Chicago and Nashville—that's where he'll be next—and we're putting together a team. We want you on it."

"How big is this?"

"Chicago, Nashville. Chicago may be tough."

"What would I have to do?"

"We'll let you know what's involved."

"Okay," I said, "but what does the project entail?"

"Chris, do you have to ask these questions? You're a member of the Church. Is it that hard a decision?"

"Well—" I started to say.

Mitsuko shook her head. "Chris, you need to be more principled."

"How's that?"

"You need to accept the will of Father. You're questioning it."

"All right. When do I start?"

"Two weeks. We'll let you know."

"Fine."

"By the way, at the White House reception tonight, I'll introduce you to someone we need to work on."

"Fine."

"You did know you were going to the reception tonight, didn't you?"

"Yes," I replied. "I was told of it."

"See you, Chris," Mitsuko said, and she left.

Part of my job was to lobby without really lobbying. The FLF, being a nonprofit organization, had no lobbying rights. If Moonies were to wield influence and power in Washington, they had to do it discreetly.

This day I had to devise a way of contacting two senators concerning a defense appropriations bill. We wanted them to support additional aid to Southeast Asia. They were borderline and we needed to tip them over on the right side.

I decided to compose a letter signed "American Youth for a Just

Peace," a letter indicating to the senators that there was within their constituency a vast group that was very much in favor of spending additional monies on Viet Nam. If that didn't work, I could perhaps search out the senators' aides at the White House gala that night and mention some things—discreetly, of course. White House receptions and parties were not the occasions to do business, but a lot of business got done there anyway.

By midafternoon, the most important task of all had not yet been done. Over coffee, then, I talked with an aide of Senator Kendall. Kendall was an archconservative from the South and respected in Congress for his strong, unwavering, intelligent stand against Communism.

"*The Rising Tide*," I was saying, "is, as you know, a publication that holds to many of the same positions your Senator holds. In fact, I can't think of a single issue on which we differ."

"Busing," the aide replied quickly. He was a sharp one.

"Well, that," I said. "Well, we don't take a stand on that."

"Why not?"

"It's not our concern. Our paper—well, you've read it—is alarmed by the spread of Communism, as is Senator Kendall. And our articles have to do with defense issues."

"And what do you want?" the aide replied, rather coldly.

"An endorsement on our front page—"

"Out of the question."

"—and we want Senator Kendall to speak at one of our banquets."

"Chris," the aide said, "you well know that Capitol Hill is teeming with folks who want something from people who have something. What is it you want and what is it I have?"

"I told you," I replied.

"And I don't believe you."

"We want more recognition. Respect."

"But who are you *really*?" the aide asked.

"Well, I'll tell you. *The Rising Tide* is part of FLF—Freedom Leadership Foundation."

"And what is that?"

"What is anything around here?" I said. "People who want something to be done differently."

The aide laughed. He was loosening up.

"All you have to know about is the paper," I said. "You've seen it. We want an endorsement. We can give your Senator's views primary exposure. You increase our exposure; we'll increase your influence."

"I don't know."

"Think about it. Don't decide now. Take a week."

The aide sighed. "I'll see what I can do. The Senator has mentioned that he needs additional publicity. He has to get the appropriations bill through. Maybe we can get something together. No promises, though."

"Fine."

"I'll get back to you."

"Great," I said. "Oh, one other thing."

"What's that?"

"What about the banquet?"

The aide shook his head. "Chris," he said, "forget the banquet."

"Forget the banquet?"

"Forget the banquet."

That night, as I took tea and pastries in the Blue Room of the White House, it struck me that I should be out on the streets selling flowers and raising money. It's part of the strange character of the Unification Church that such a differentiation in life-style is possible.

Life for me had in Washington become a lot more plush and sophisticated. Washington Moonies still led a strict, structured existence, but we lived in Georgetown townhouses and wore expensive clothes. In fact, we did sell flowers occasionally, but traveled far away to do so, in order not to be recognized by those we were trying to woo on Capitol Hill.

Several rooms in the White House had been opened up for the reception. History oozed from the woodwork; the furnishings, paintings, and antiques all told stories of power and the past. I was enthralled—and it wasn't even my first time here. White House galas were always special, yet still quite common.

I could hear the military string ensemble playing something in another room. The tinkle of fine china cups and saucers and a chatter of silver made the place seem lively; people stood in pairs or threes talking loudly and laughing.

Mitsuko emerged from the East Room and walked up to me.

"Hello," she said, smiling cheerfully.

"Hello," I replied. I remembered my new task: organizing pro-Nixon rallies in Chicago and Nashville. I had learned elsewhere that

Mitsuko was aiming to hold rallies in every one of the fifty states, each to be held on the steps of that state's capitol. There was an all-out effort to secure support for Nixon. Every day now Family members distributed petitions that endorsed the President. Often they would offer small gifts to gain friendship and to receive notice from busy, bustling congressmen.

"Chris," Mitsuko said. "I want you to meet someone. This is Jack from the Young Americans for Freedom." Mitsuko nodded to me slightly and smiled quickly.

"Jack," she went on, "this is Chris Elkins from Freedom Leadership Foundation."

This was delicate. There were several issues that the YAF and FLF agreed upon—military strength, anti-Communism, nationalism. And often the two organizations had participated side-by-side in certain projects. But the FLF had a working relationship with the Young Socialists, and if anyone from YAF found out, it would spell disaster. At FLF you had to walk a tightrope. As Moonies, we dealt with anyone who could benefit us, and often the groups we supported were violently opposed in theory and ideology to each other.

"It's good to meet you," I said to Jack.

"And it's a pleasure to meet you," he said to me. "Haven't we met before somewhere?"

"I don't think so," I replied. "Well, were you at the Hungarian Freedom Fighter's dinner where our newspaper received an award?"

"No, it wouldn't have been there, but perhaps it was David's testimonial."

"That's it!" I said.

"Yes, I knew I had seen you before."

"Say, I have a project you might be interested in."

"Oh, what's that?"

"Well, it's a Nixon thing," I said.

"Can we talk about it?" he asked.

"Not here. I'll catch you sometime this week."

It was always just that sort of thing. Developing contacts, referring them to other people who could use them, stringing them along, keeping them alive and ready to be tapped at a moment's notice. Although we Moonies were relatively new at intricacies of Washington wheeling and dealing, we were getting good at it. We worked at it harder than anyone else.

I saw Neil Salonen in the East Room. We had always envisioned Salonen someday becoming President. Our Washington work and the keen interest of the Church in national politics led me to think that perhaps there was more political strategy in the Church than I had at first thought, and that somehow Salonen was in the thick of it. Once, Moon said that if present-day senators and congressmen didn't respond to him, he would have to create his own.

I walked beside Salonen and we looked out over the crowd.

"Looking over your prospective residence?" I asked.

Salonen's aide, Dan, scolded me quickly, "Not so loud!" He turned to see if anyone had heard.

Salonen just smiled and said, "How are you doing, Chris?"

"Just fine. It's good to see you."

"Thank you." He stood up. "Let's take a look around."

We wandered through, looking at the place, the paintings, the people. Salonen didn't say much. And then, quickly, he had to leave. He didn't want to stay long for fear of being recognized. Since we had started the Nixon support, Salonen's name had gotten a lot of press, mostly bad. He would stay out of sight now for a while.

Senator Kendall's aide stopped me in the Blue Room. I had just picked up some more tea. "Want some?" I asked.

"No, thanks," the aide replied. "I just have time to tell you that we'll have something for you next week."

"Great. I appreciate it."

"We'll get front page?"

"Front page," I said. "Oh, one other thing."

He smiled. "Chris," he said. "No banquet."

"No banquet?"

"No banquet."

Later, standing on the south portico of the White House, I looked over the perfectly manicured lawns to the Washington Monument just beyond the clear rippling blue of the tidal basin. About halfway between was the "Washington, D.C. Holy Ground." Moonies often met there in the wee hours of the morning to pray and sing. Being so close to the White House we'd attract police. We'd tell them that we were a church group meeting there to pray. "You want to join us?" we'd ask. They usually let us be.

A friend from FLF, named Ray, stepped beside me.

"Enjoying yourself?" he asked.

"Sure," I replied.

"Me too."

"It's all a dream, isn't it?"

Ray sighed. "I wish my parents could see me now," he said.

"Me too," I answered. "Me too."

13

January 1975
Washington/New York

During my months in Washington I hadn't much time to think. The schedule was as hectic as ever, and I was realizing that this was the course of life in the Unification Church, whether one sold candles or "influence." There was always something urgent to be done, and it was strongly communicated that individual effort, or rather, lack of it, could be the hand of Satan sabotaging the movement's divine mission.

By now I was living on Military Road in northwest Washington, and I was managing the staff of the Ginseng Teahouse. I had been transferred away from FLF because of a conflict with one person there, and I had desired to move on because of personal doubts concerning the direction of the political wing of the movement after Nixon's resignation. I had been sent to work in some congressional campaigns for a while, and I had participated in Moon's Madison Square Garden Rally in September.

Now I was enjoying the work at the teahouse. It was a new venture of the Unification Church and everyone had hopes that it would turn into a chain restaurant operation. We served Moon's ginseng tea, the Il Hwa brand, and we prepared health food lunches. We had a staff of twelve but hired some waitresses from outside in hopes of winning them to the movement.

I kept busy, but not quite as busy as I had been at FLF. Certain doubts crept into my head, especially about Moon. At times, the only thing which confirmed my faith in the Unification Church was the conviction that there were no other alternatives—my parents hadn't trusted in me, I felt, and the church Christianity that I had known before wasn't a Christianity of commitment and action as this was. And it certainly didn't manifest the sort of love that I experienced with my Moonie brothers and sisters.

I learned that other Moonie friends had doubts too, but that they were stronger than I because they had spent more time studying the Divine Principle. They had moved up in the Church more slowly than I had. Moon had captured my heart and will, but it seemed that his grasp on my mind was not quite so firm.

Once I was sent on an errand that challenged my feelings about Moon and the Church. I was called out in the middle of the night to buy a birthday present for one of Moon's children. At first I thought it was a joke. But as it was explained to me, I realized that this was a serious and important project.

Keith, an administrative aide, was telling me, "We know that Father has been wanting to get the children a dog and is really fond of Norwegian elkhounds. Since they are rare and extremely expensive we feel that the best bet of finding one fast will be in New York City."

I still did not see how this all tied in with me. Why not get someone in New York to get the dog and take it out to Moon?

Neil Salonen explained, "We need someone to do the job quickly and efficiently. If the gift arrives after noon, it will seem as if we have forgotten the birthday. Since I can depend on you to do a job well, I want you to fly to New York on the next available flight and find an elkhound."

Then, half jokingly and half seriously, he said, "And who could better find a good elkhound than someone named Elkins?"

I dutifully chuckled at the humor, but I knew that he was serious. "Sure," I said, "I'll be on the next plane." Paul, the Unification Church treasurer, handed me an envelope with several fifty dollar bills in it and asked me to turn in all of the receipts.

On the way back to the Center, I heard a voice behind me. "Excuse me, sir."

I wheeled around to find a clean-cut young man with a bucket of carnations under his arm. I knew that he was one of our fund raisers on a mobile team, but catching me off guard the way he did gave him the opportunity to continue his sale before I could say anything.

"I am working with an interdenominational youth group raising money for missions," he continued.

I decided to play along. "Oh," I said. "And what is the money used for?"

"We're using it to help kids on drugs and to start mission work around the world to help people," he enthusiastically told me. I had to work at keeping a straight face. This was the first time I had ever been on the *receiving* end of a fund raiser.

Coyly I asked, "Is this connected with Reverend Moon in any way?" I knew that that was the hardest question to answer. To say yes would kill the sale, to say no would be a lie too easy to be caught in.

"We support many churches," he said. "We just want to share God's love with everyone."

"And all of this money is used for mission work?" I asked, knowing what he would say.

"Yes, sir!" he said, almost straightening up to attention.

"You do an excellent job at fund raising," I replied. A bewildered look formed on his face. I laughed. "I, too, am a Family member," I said. "If I hadn't been, you would have had me sold."

As we bid each other good-bye I almost told him about the mission I was being sent on. I am sure that he had no idea that the several hundred dollars that he worked eighteen hours a day, seven days a week to earn would be spent on a dog for Moon. Although he would not have questioned the expenditure openly, in his mind it would have indeed raised doubts. I chose to let him remain naive.

Once in New York, I quickly started phoning. Elkhounds were hard to find and soon I realized that I would not be able to get the dog to Moon by the middle of the day. But I continued, knowing that Salonen would want a gift to get there no matter how late.

I finally found a dog in Greenwich Village at a rather posh pet shop. Filling out the papers, I had to disclose to the clerk who would own the pet.

"The name of the owner?" the clerk asked me.

I paused for a second and obviously was hesitant about saying it. Suddenly everyone around seemed to be listening. "Let me spell it for you," I said. "S-u-n M-y-u-n-g M-o-o-n."

I could feel the atmosphere grow thick. Although the clerk did not say anything at first, she looked as if she had become frozen.

She looked up and said, "Is this who I think it is?"

"I don't know," I answered. "Who do you think it is?"

"The guy with the posters up all over the city. The Korean guru," she said.

"Well, yes and no. He is the guy with posters up everywhere, but he is not a guru."

"Do you believe in him?" she asked. By this time a small crowd had gathered around me.

That question always sent me into a tailspin. I knew deep down that I still had major doubts, yet after being in for several months I had an obligation to answer yes.

"That's a long story," I said, trying to evade the question. "I am a member of the Unification Church, which is a Moon organization."

A lady standing nearby asked, "Well, don't all of you believe that he is the messiah—the return of Christ?"

I found myself automatically giving the answer I had been trained to say. "We believe that he is perhaps a prophet, much like a John the Baptist figure, preparing the way for Christ's return."

"That's not what I have read," she said.

"Do you believe everything you read?" I asked.

"Of course not," she said, trapping herself.

"Then, I suggest if you want to know who Moon is and what we believe, that you come see for yourself." Obviously this frustrated her.

"Well," she said in a last ditch effort, "I believe in the Bible."

"Good," I said, "so do I. And in it you will find instructions to judge a tree by its fruit."

By this time she was flustered, and rather than argue any further she simply turned and walked away. Although visibly I had won the encounter, I felt inside that I had been deceptive, and it disturbed me.

By the time I got the dog it was two o'clock. I rented a car and immediately left for East Garden, the estate where Moon lived in Irvington, New York. If I made good time, I would be there by three.

Once I arrived, the guards at the gate were hesitant to let me in. They had not been informed to expect me, and until someone from the main house gave clearance I wouldn't get further than the gate. The security around Moon was always tight.

Daikon, Moon's driver, was at the main house, and when told of the purpose of my visit he gave permission for me to come in. By the time I reached the front drive, Daikon was there to meet me.

He was a very pleasant man, quite trusted, and extremely close to Moon. "Hello," he said, making his *l*'s sound like *r*'s. "You have gift for Hye-Jin?"

"Yes," I said gleefully. "We have a Norwegian elkhound puppy for her from the American Church. May I present it to Father?"

"I think maybe not," he said in his Oriental English. "Father expect gift this morning. Maybe I should take to him." At that he disappeared into the house for what seemed to be hours.

When he returned, he still had the puppy in his hands and motioned for me to walk with him over to the garage. Daikon was in charge of Moon's cars and he slept in a small apartment above the garage. Upon entering the garage, I noticed the limousine and the Mercedes Benz. Daikon told me that Moon had a sports car too, which was being repaired.

He put the puppy down and said, "Father would not receive puppy. But, I keep him here and soon Father will love him."

The puppy playfully ran around the garage while Daikon and I talked. The more I considered the situation, the angrier I became. I had spent most of the night and all that day finding that dog. Besides spending a fortune on it, my airplane ticket and car rental had made the venture quite expensive. And for him not to receive me and then to reject the gift only further increased the growing conflicts in my mind.

"We'll need at least fifteen San Juaquins and probably ten Poconos," I said, referring to our teahouse sandwiches. We spent most evenings preparing the food for the next day. While talking in the kitchen, I heard the jingle of the bell on the front door signaling that someone had come in. Assuming it was a customer thinking we were open, I walked toward the front of the restaurant to tell him we were closed.

To my surprise I found Randy Remmel, the choir director. "Randy!" I said as I ran to embrace him, "It's so good to see you." We laughed and talked for a few minutes and I asked him in for a cup of tea, which he gladly accepted.

We sat down in a quiet corner of the restaurant and began to talk. I was pretty much running the teahouse myself now and was worse for the wear. Often half of the staff would be called off on a special mission at the last minute and leave the rest of us to try to handle the situation. Many times we almost crumbled during the heavy lunch rushes. Keeping up the morale of the staff when I could hardly keep up my own morale was getting more difficult. Randy was a breath of fresh air for me, someone I could talk to.

Randy reached across the table, put his hand on my shoulder, and said, "How are you doing, Elk? I mean really deep inside, how are you doing?"

Randy had a way of reaching down inside me, going beyond the facade that I often put up for everyone else. Just calling me "Elk" made me comfortable with him and reminded me of our abiding trust in each other.

I opened my mouth to respond, but words did not come out. Suddenly my eyes were flooded with tears, and great sobs began to well up inside of me. For several minutes all I could do was cry. Randy sat there and soothed me and told me not to feel bad about crying and just to let it all out. He knew that I had been under a great deal of pressure.

Once I gained my composure I said, "Randy, I don't know why that happened. I had everything under control until you asked about it. But, things are pretty rough. We are expected to make this restaurant an ideal business, yet I can never be sure from day to day if we will have enough people to run it. We are behind on our bills because we have been using Teahouse funds to support other church activities, and sometimes I feel the weight of all of this on my shoulders."

Randy smiled sympathetically. "But you and I both know that that is not the biggest problem you have," he said.

Knowing what he meant, yet afraid to admit it, I asked him, "What do you mean?"

"All of us are asked to do the work of a dozen people everyday in half the time, and unless we have absolute faith in the True Parents none of us will ever make it."

"I know what you mean," I said, looking down at the floor.

"Chris," he said. "Don't think that you are the only one having doubts. If we had all of us together at one time, over half of us would seriously doubt the validity of our actions. If we did not need each other so badly, many of us would leave."

There was a long period of silence between us. Several times we had been interrupted by teahouse staffers asking me questions. Randy began to see how trapped I felt. At that moment I felt the business would fall apart if I left it. No one seemed to know it any better than I did.

"We're going to get you out of this. You need to get more involved in the Principle and learn it better," Randy said. "We'll take care of you, Chris."

At the time I thought that what he was saying was impossible. Who could take over? It would take months for someone to learn the ropes.

Three days later I was packing my bags to move on to a new mission. A whole new staff was being organized for the teahouse, since most of us were burned out and needed a change. It amazed me how fast things could change in the Family. One day could make all the difference in your attitude about the Church.

With the prospect of a new mission, I once again was enthused. Randy had encouraged me to call my parents, to tell them of the change, and to sound happy and confident to them. Although my contacts with them were sometimes months apart, I did enjoy speaking with them. They were encouraging me about coming home to spend more time with them.

My new mission was with the College Association for the Research of Principles (CARP) at American University in Washington D.C. I was glad to be staying in Washington; I had really grown to love the city. Marc Lee, Salonen's assistant, was also transferred there and was once again my most immediate leader.

Every weekend we sponsored workshops at a lodge in Virginia. Rarely would we have less than ten students from American University to go, and we were sure that we could win the favor of at least half of them.

Workshops always began on Friday evenings after class. We would arrange a central place to meet all of those who had signed up to go. Often we advertised in the school newspaper, "Wanted: People concerned about their fellow men. Learn how to make the world a better place. Contact . . . " We received surprisingly good responses.

The purpose of the workshop was to bring a "little bit of the kingdom of heaven to earth." Although there was quite a bit of lecturing over the two-day event, it included everything from nature hikes to square dancing. The food was bountiful and delicious. Harmony and love seemed to abound everywhere.

One weekend Jane came to our workshop. We had found her on

the streets of Georgetown. She was naive, yet terribly sensitive to the harshness of the world around her.

One Friday evening, after all of the participants found their bunks and bedded down for the night, we conference leaders quietly met and discussed each newcomer individually.

"What about Jane?" Marc asked.

"She's perfect," someone said. "She already thinks that we are terrific. She is easily influenced by others though, and we need to keep her away from a couple of the more negative people."

Marc thought for a moment. "Jeff and Ron seem to be the most negative," he said. "Didn't they say that they were going to get up and go on a hike in the morning before breakfast?"

"Yes," I replied. "Jane said she wanted to go with them, too."

"I don't like that situation. Chris, you get up and go with them in the morning to be sure they don't become too negative. Right now, Jane is our best prospect, and we don't want her unduly influenced by Jeff and Ron."

After discussing a few more of the guests, we prayed together and broke up the meeting. Some of the girls who were doing the cooking had to start preparing the next day's food. They might not get to sleep at all that night.

I walked out into the brisk night air. The lodge we stayed in was surrounded by tall pine trees, and a small, babbling creek ran right in front. The air was clean and only the night noises were to be heard.

The lodge was a pleasant place to go each weekend. I got to hear the Principle lectured and helped lead others into the church. It was amazing what we could do in a short two-day period. Some people were willing to change their whole life-style after one weekend with us.

That night, though, I wanted to walk out to the road and just be alone. I had been in the movement for over two years and I still had some of the doubts about the movement that I had had when I first joined. Being alone helped me sort through them.

By the time I crossed the rickety bridge over the creek that led out to the main road, I could hear noises other than crickets and frogs. The unmistakable noise of a car a mile down the road caught my attention. One did not just happen to drive by the lodge—any cars on the road knew where they were going.

As the headlights came over the hill I noticed that the car was a police car. My heart began to pound rapidly as the beams of the headlights blinded me. I knew I had to act calm; but the last thing we needed was the police.

The car pulled up beside me and someone inside shined a flashlight in my eyes. "Lost?" a voice from inside the car inquired.

"No," I answered, shielding my eyes from the light. "Are you?" Immediately, I was sorry I asked that. But no one answered my question.

"Well then, maybe you can help us," one policeman asked. "We are looking for the Moonie, er, Unification camp out here. Do you know where it is?"

"Yes," I said politely. "I am in the meeting out here. What do you want?"

"Is there a girl named Jane Pollack here this weekend?"

At first I did not know how to answer. I did not want to make them angry or suspicious, but I also didn't feel they had the right to know.

"Why do you need to know?" I asked.

"Her mother died tonight."

Without hesitating I said, "Why don't you follow me, and I'll get her for you. You'll have to park out here. The bridge won't sustain the weight of your car." They followed me in. The two policemen seemed tense. I guess they didn't know what to expect.

I first woke up Marc to tell him what had happened. He told me to stall the officers while he went to wake up Jane.

When Jane and Marc appeared in the front room I was surprised that Jane was so well composed. I had assumed that Marc must not have told her.

"You are Jane Pollack?" the officer asked.

"Yes," she said.

"We regret to inform you that your mother passed away tonight. Your father asked us to find you and bring you in," the officer explained.

"When is the funeral?" Jane asked, expressionless.

"Sunday afternoon."

"Well," Jane said, "I am not going to go back tonight. Tell my father I will contact him tomorrow." (Our phone at the lodge did not work.)

The officers looked a little puzzled and asked her if she was sure.

She calmly told them that yes she was sure. Shrugging their shoulders, they bid us a good night and left. I was sitting there with my mouth open.

"I am so sorry, Jane," I said.

"She's been sick quite a while," Jane said.

I could see that her mind was just beginning to absorb the news.

"Mr. Lee," she said to Marc, "I think that you are right. Satan is trying to take me away from here. He is using my mother's death to try to draw me away."

I couldn't believe what I was hearing. This girl's mother had just died, and Marc had convinced her that Satan was using the death to draw her away from us.

"Which is more important to you, Jane?" Marc asked. "God or this physical world?"

"God," Jane answered.

"This is the most important weekend of your life. You will have to choose whether you will follow God or follow the world. You must be awfully important to Satan for him to use something so desperate to try to get you back," Marc said.

"Do you really think so?"

"If you can remain faithful through this, God will have great things in store for you. You must not go for any reason now."

"Oh, thank you, Mr. Lee," she said. But, I could see tears in her eyes. The longer we stood there in the silence, the harder she fought back the sorrow she needed to express.

"Be strong," Marc whispered. "We are your family."

14

December 1975
New York/Carlsbad

I had been selected to be editor of the *World Student Times*, the major CARP publication. The paper was being started from scratch and I had been given a big responsibility. The staff would be located in New York. Although I had been to New York City several times, I had never lived there for any length of time. The city was exciting, but I felt that the life-style was inhibiting.

Rarely did a day go by that I did not see or hear Moon. Yet, rather than being positive in its effect, it had caused me to doubt more. Moon struck me as being a man interested in one thing—results. Your methods were not important, only your results. Being placed so close to Moon forced me continually to face my doubts.

Never did I let on to Mom and Dad about my doubts for fear that they were looking for me to crack. Though their often expressed, steadfast position was affecting me, causing me to think things through and to have second thoughts about my actions, Mom and Dad seemed quite discouraged about it all; they must have thought they weren't getting through to me.

Still, we kept in touch by phone. Mom informed me that my brother Ned was getting married December 19, and she wanted me there for the wedding. I wanted to attend, and I said that, yes, I would be there. Of course, I had no idea whether the Center would grant me permission.

My new leader was Tom. He and I got along well, and he allowed me a great deal of freedom in my work on the newspaper. Since I wrote most of it, did all of the layout and editing, it required a great deal of time. Rarely did I have to fund raise, which I took to be a blessing.

Confronting Tom about going home for the wedding would not be easy. Although he appreciated my family situation, he was adamantly loyal to Moon. Yet, more than once did Tom and I slip away from the others and go to a movie or go fishing. In the movement one was always left with the impression that while you were out fundraising in the pouring rain, your leader was working twice as hard somewhere else. Once I myself had become a leader, I found that this was rarely true.

One afternoon I found Tom in a good mood and since we were alone in the Center I asked, "Tom, what would you think if I wanted to go home for my brother's wedding?"

He raised his eyebrows, half smiled, and said, "I think that you know what I would think." He paused. "When is he getting married?"

"December 19."

"That's awfully close to Christmas. I've already told the members that none of us are going to go home for the holidays. They may think that I am letting you have special privileges."

About the time that I thought he was going to say no he said, "Let me think about it."

I knew that that was a good sign. At least he was considering it a possibility.

For several days I had been going down to the firm that printed our newspaper in order to work on some layout ideas. With Ned's marriage on my mind and my constant, nagging doubts about the Church, I would often spend time in Central Park just walking and thinking.

I had heard Moon say that he was greater than Jesus and that Jesus had even bowed to him. As well, I had recently been told that Moon had married Jesus to a Korean woman. Aside from the fact that I had been told that Jesus' physical father was Zacharias (the father of John the Baptist) much of the teachings about Jesus had changed radically from those I first heard when I joined the movement.

I would sometimes find a quiet little spot in Central Park and lie

120

down and look up in the sky wondering if all of this was really happening to me. I could be isolated there from the rumble of the city and the hassle of the Church and just think. As much as I wanted to believe that the Family was good and righteous, the heart of the movement I considered to be blasphemous. Yet, I felt so loved that leaving often seemed beyond the realm of possibility. I often wondered during those hours spent in Central Park if I had been brainwashed.

On one particular afternoon I decided that I was going home for Ned's wedding whether Tom said I could or not. Although it scared me to think of bucking the system, inside I knew that I couldn't possibly miss that wedding.

Tom called me into his office one day. He was sitting at a desk, and looked up at me and said, "You can go. But you must not stay for Christmas. You will be needed here for the newspaper. Besides, I am not letting any of the others go to their parents' for Christmas."

I was elated inside. Yet, too, I was bewildered. Why had he gone against the Principle and let me go?

"Why did you say yes, Tom?" I asked later.

Without even looking up he said, "I knew that you would go whether I said yes or not. At least this way I am sure you will come back."

I thought, "How did he know?" Tom's perception was good, but I thought I had been hiding my feeling rather well of late. I guess not, though. I was glad, however, that he did not force me to go against his will. Yet, he was right, too. I knew I would come back no matter what.

I had forgotten how desolate New Mexico looked in the winter. There are no trees or tall buildings—nothing to obstruct the panoramic view of the desert. It was a landscape full of loneliness those days, especially since it was Christmas. Christmas in Carlsbad never seemed festive. There was never any snow and usually the wind picked up and blew dust in the air and everyone's allergies would flare up.

Mom and Dad didn't know that I planned to leave before Christmas Day. They assumed that I would stay after the wedding was over.

I took a shuttle into Carlsbad. I had not told Mom and Dad when I would arrive. Since it was December 18th—the day of the wedding rehearsal—I am sure that they had begun to doubt that I would arrive at all.

I walked from the bus depot on Canal Street over to the junior high school where my mother taught. I knew she would be excited to see me. I slipped into a side door of the building, avoiding the front office, and walked down to Mother's classroom. She had a class in session, but I peeked in anyway.

"Chrissie," she blurted out in full voice. As she embraced me she said, crying, "I was so afraid that you weren't coming."

"I told you that I'd be here. I'm just cutting it a little close," I joked.

"A little close! The rehearsal is in less than three hours."

"I wasn't sure when I would be able to come in. Why don't you go on back to class and I'll see you later." She embraced me again and told me how glad she was that I was home.

We were never a very affectionate family. We loved each other but we rarely expressed it in physical ways. Mother's outpouring of affection seemed to me to be a bit out of character, but I knew she was glad to see me and I didn't think anything else of it.

I took her car and drove on home. My brother Ned was there when I arrived. "Nothing like keeping us in suspense," he said, shaking my hand. "I was afraid I was going to have to find someone your size to fit into your tux."

I laughed. "Not a chance," I said. "I wouldn't miss seeing you get tied down for the world!"

Ned and I had grown close since he had graduated from high school. Although I am sure that he didn't condone my Unification Church activity, he never criticized me about it. I always felt comfortable around him.

The hustle and bustle of the rehearsal and dinner allowed my late arrival to go unnoticed by most everyone else. During the evening I would look at the people involved in the wedding and wonder just how much they knew about me. I couldn't tell from Mom and Dad's actions how many people they had told about me.

I was not surprised, though, when their pastor, Brother Walt, took an interest in me. I considered his interest in me only to be something Mom and Dad had asked him to do.

"What's a New Mexico boy like you doing living in New York City?" he asked me.

In answering, I wasn't sure what he knew and whether or not he was testing my honesty. "I am editing a newspaper called the *World Student Times*," I said. "It's for a Christian student organization."

Brother Walt had come to Carlsbad after I left for college and so we didn't really know each other. His additional questions led me to believe that he knew nothing more about me.

Brother Walt and I spent the evening together talking in a corner while the rest of the people at the dinner were laughing and having a good time. His sincerity impressed me. I felt a close kinship to the events that led him into the ministry. Although not very educated, he had a heart of gold and was genuinely concerned about what I was doing. He never mentioned Moon and neither did I.

Mother and Dad had been particularly hospitable. I wasn't sure if it was because of the wedding or if they were warming up to me. Although I had been having serious doubts about my involvement in the Unification Church I dared not breathe a word of it to them. I didn't want to argue or have to defend the Church. And, surprisingly enough, they didn't bring it up either.

They gave me the use of their credit cards and charge accounts to buy gifts for Christmas. The atmosphere was cheerful and homey. And after the wedding, I didn't want to go back to New York immediately, so I decided to stay for a few extra days, still thinking that I would leave before Christmas.

But I was surprised not to receive any calls from Tom. Any other time that I had been away my leader had always called me at least every other day. I decided that Tom wasn't calling on purpose, so to teach me a lesson of some kind, or to determine if I was principled enough to call him.

As Christmas grew nearer, I knew I was facing a showdown. If I stayed home through Christmas, I knew that I might decide not to go back. The silence from New York made me feel that I was being tested. I again thought of how Satan might be trying to woo me out of the Church. Yet somehow that reasoning did not seem good anymore.

On the afternoon of December 23 I rounded the corner in front of Parchman-Carver hardware store on my way to Gerrell's men's store. The wind was blowing the already skimpy Christmas decorations to pieces. The wind was warm and full of dust, and somehow it just did not seem like Christmas.

To my amazement, across the street in front of Jackson's drug store was Travis. He was with his sister and brother-in-law and it looked like they were window shopping. I slipped up behind them in order to surprise Travis. We had not seen each other in months.

"Guess who," I said, putting my hands over his eyes.

"Chris," he said, spinning around. "So good to see you."

"You too," I said. "What are you doing here?"

"My family is in Roswell visiting," he answered. "I was just going to look you up. I knew you were here." In a more somber tone, he added, "We really need to get together—and real soon, too."

I didn't know exactly what he meant, but I said, "Sure. Why don't we go out to Sambo's and talk there."

"Let me finish my shopping with Gary and Louise first, and let's meet here in an hour," Travis said.

"Fine," I replied. "See you in an hour."

I walked away, wondering what could be weighing so heavy on his mind. We had always held the confidence of each other in highest regard, and we knew we could tell each other anything without fear of rejection. I couldn't imagine what was so important.

An hour later we met and I drove him out to Sambo's. We shared a little chit-chat at the beginning, but my curiosity was killing me.

"Travis, what is it that you have to tell me?" I asked curiously.

For a few seconds he just looked at me without saying a word. "Maybe we better wait until you're not driving," he said.

"I can handle it," I replied.

"You're not going to like this."

"Well, tell me. I can't stand it any longer."

"The other night I tried to call your Mom and Dad to find out if you were going to be home for Christmas. I got a recording saying that your phone number was no longer a working number."

"Our number? We have had it for twenty years!"

"Yeah," Travis said, "I know. So, I called Jay to ask him what was going on. I thought maybe your folks had moved and I didn't know about it." Suddenly Travis just stopped talking and looked out the window.

"Well," I said, "go on!"

"Chris, I am betraying your parents' confidence by telling you this. Maybe I shouldn't."

"Tell me!" I almost shouted.

"Jay gave me the new number. It is unlisted."

"That's why I haven't heard from anyone in New York," I said, thinking out loud. By this time we had arrived at Sambo's. We walked inside and picked up the story once we were settled into a booth.

"Jay encouraged me to call your parents," Travis continued. "He said something very important was happening and that they would probably want to hear from me. So, I called them. At first, your mom couldn't believe that I had gotten the number. Then I told her Jay had given it to me and told me to call."

I interjected, "I think I know what you're getting ready to tell me."

"Maybe so, but let me finish. Your mom said that they had decided the only way to ever get you out of the Moonies was to hire deprogrammers. And since you were going to come home for the wedding, this would be the perfect time."

"What did they want you to do?" I asked.

"Just to cooperate in keeping you at home long enough for the deprogrammers to get here."

Hearing Travis was like finding the hidden key to a puzzle. I suddenly realized why I had gotten no calls from New York and why Mom and Dad had been so cooperative. I realized too that all of my friends in the area had entertained me just to cooperate with the deprogramming effort. It was like being stabbed in the back.

"Travis," I began after a few moments of silence, staring out the window. "Who all is involved in this?"

"I don't know," he said. "Jay knows. Although I don't think that he agrees with what is going on, he feels pressured, like I do, to help. But, I don't know of anyone else."

I thought of Brother Walt. Although he hadn't said a word I suspected that he knew. Every day since I had been home we had gotten together to share thoughts and views with each other. At that point I assumed that everyone was involved.

"When is this going to happen—the deprogramming? I asked.

"I don't know that either," Travis answered.

"We have got to find out. Why don't you call Jay and fish for the information?"

Travis walked over to a pay phone and talked with Jay for several minutes. The whole time he was gone I thought over my options. Only one seemed viable. I knew I would have to escape before the deprogrammers got there. The only place to go would be back to

New York. Suddenly my differences with the Unification Church melted away. I was forced to go there.

Travis approached the table grim-faced. He sat down and said, "We think it's going to happen on Christmas Day. Probably less than thirty-six hours."

15

Christmas 1975/ January 1976
Carlsbad/New York/Atlanta

"Come in, Travis," Mother said with a smile. "I think Chris is back in his bedroom." I was quietly and inconspicuously packing.

"Chrissie," Mother called out, "Travis is here." I heard Travis say hello to my father as he headed back toward my bedroom. Afraid that Mother might be with him, I stuffed my luggage into the closet.

There was a soft knock at the door. "Come in," I said.

"Hi," Travis said, rolling his eyes back to indicate that Mother was right behind him.

"What are you boys going to do today?" Mother asked cheerfully.

"I think that we're going to go to the Red Chimney and eat some barbeque for lunch, if Travis wants to," I replied.

"Let me get you some money." Mother clearly wasn't aware that I knew what was going on. She disappeared down the hall.

After talking to Jay the day before, Travis and I decided the best way to escape fast would be to try to get me on the last eastbound plane departing at 12:30 P.M. It was Christmas Eve, and Mom and Dad thought their plans were going to be successful. We knew that we would have to be discreet, so I masterminded the whole event using Travis as a blind.

Whispering, I said, "Travis, get both Mom and Dad in the kitchen while I sneak my suitcases out to Dad's pickup. Hurry. We have less than two hours.

He winked at me and walked on down the hall, and I could hear

Mom and Dad and Travis talking in the kitchen. Quietly I tiptoed down the hall, slipped through the den and out the sliding glass doors to the pickup parked behind the back fence. I had packed everything I possibly could into two small suitcases. I wasn't sure that I would ever be back again.

I went back into the house the same way and went into the kitchen where we all talked for several minutes. I had bought several Christmas gifts the day before to give further indication that I was planning to stay through Christmas. But, I purposely left one gift unpurchased.

"Before we go eat," I said to Travis, "I still have to buy one more gift. Why don't we go now so we can get the gift and get to the Red Chimney before the rush."

"That's fine with me."

"Do you have enough money?" Dad asked.

"I have plenty," I said. "Can we take the pickup, Dad?"

"Sure," he replied. "Are you sure that you don't want to take the car?"

"You two might want it. I'd just as soon drive the pickup."

"We'll see you later," Travis said to Mom and Dad.

"When do you think that you'll be home?" Mom asked, trying not to sound too suspicious. I had realized since yesterday how close they were keeping track of me.

"Probably around one."

"Okay. See you then."

About the time we got to the pickup, I heard the sliding glass door open. We had just begun to think that we had pulled it off. Dad came out and said, "That ol' pickup is hard to start. Want me to do it for you?" he asked as he headed toward us.

Trying not to panic, I said, "Oh, I think that between the two of us we'll manage to get it going." I knew that if he even came to the fence he would see my suitcases.

"Okay," he said throwing his hands up, and he turned to go back in.

"That was close," I muttered.

"He would kill us, especially me, if he found out," Travis said. That was one thing that I had worried about—Travis's safety. I knew that my parents would be violently angry and I feared for Travis after I was gone. I had Travis park his car at my brother's apartment so that once I was on the plane he could drive the pickup back there, get his car, and leave town immediately. And the pickup would be in a place where it would easily be found by my parents once I was gone.

We went downtown for a few minutes just in case Dad and Mom were following us. Soon it was obvious that they were not, and we sped to the airport, about thirty minutes away. The airport was small and only one airline served it. Often the planes were late, but that day they ran on time. When we arrived, the plane was already on the ground.

Not much was said between us until we got in sight of the airport. Travis asked, "What are you going to do now?"

"I really don't know," I said. "First of all, I'll go back to New York tonight. But, I'm not sure that is where I want to be."

"You know that you always have a home with me, Chris."

I smiled and said, "Thanks, I'll remember that."

I drove the pickup to the front of the terminal and did not even shut off the engine. I hopped out, grabbed my luggage, and said, "You get out of here. Leave Carlsbad as soon as possible."

"Don't worry," he said, "I will."

He reached down and hugged me and for a few seconds we held each other. Then, his voice cracking, he said, "Chris, I disagree with what you and the Moonies believe, but I still love you and I don't think deprogramming is the answer. Straighten out your life and get back with your parents. They love you, too."

"Thanks," I said with tears in my eyes. "You have been a real friend."

I watched him drive off and stood for a few minutes looking around at the panorama of the desert. During those few minutes I felt I would never be able to return again.

Realizing what had to be done, I quickly turned and ran into the airport. I checked my luggage, and with five minutes left before boarding, I decided to make one last telephone call.

My finger trembled with fear as I dialed the number. The phone rang once—no answer. It rang again—still no answer. On the third ring I heard the call being answered: "Hello."

"Brother Walt?"

"Yes," he said, not knowing who he was talking to.

"This is Chris."

There was silence for a few seconds, then he asked, "Where are you?"

"That's not important," I said firmly. "I have a message I want you to relay to my parents."

I thought I heard him say, "Oh, no," under his breath, but I continued, "I have discovered what all of you have been up to. I am *not* going to be deprogrammed. I will have to work out this situation for myself."

"Chris," he begged. "Don't leave. And please don't think that I have been involved. I only found out this morning when I brought a book over for you while you were still asleep. Your Mother told me then what was going on. They had never told me anything about you until then."

"Well," I said, "I want to believe that. I really enjoyed our time together, but it is too late now. If I don't leave immediately they will kidnap me. I want you to call them and tell them that I have discovered their plot and that I have escaped."

I was sure I could hear him crying, and this made my eyes fill with tears. "Please stay, Chris," he said. "We'll work this out."

"I can't. I know that they've gone too far to back down now. You call them and give them that message. My plane leaves in a couple of minutes." I really did not intend to tell him that I was flying, but it slipped out.

"Why don't *you* call them," he said.

"Right now I don't feel like they deserve any consideration from me, and even asking you to call them is more than I originally intended to do."

"Chris," he said, "I don't think that I am going to talk you out of this."

"You're right," I quickly answered.

"I want you to know something, though," he said. "I don't agree with the Moonies, but I still love you. We're going to be praying for you."

I had often had people tell me that they were going to be praying for me, but somehow I believed that Brother Walt really would.

"Good-bye, Brother Walt," I said.

"God bless you, Chris," he said. My flight departure was being announced as I hung up. I walked straight onto the plane with tears streaming down my face. The door was closed behind me and in a matter of moments we were streaming down the runway, lifting off from the desert. As we circled back over the airport a car just like brother Walt's pulled into the airport drive.

We landed twice before arriving in Dallas two and a half hours later. I had felt every emotion. I was elated that I had escaped, afraid that I had made a wrong decision and sorrowful knowing the sorrow in my parent's home at that minute. I wondered if they would have the police waiting for me in Dallas. Brother Walt knew I was flying and they could easily figure out I was going to Dallas.

When we arrived in Dallas it was dark. I had not booked a continuing flight for fear that someone could trace me through it. There were three flights leaving within two hours, and I planned to take the last one. I felt that if anyone was trying to trace me through Dallas, they would figure I would be on the next flight out to New York. I hid in a bathroom till flight time.

As usual, we had to go through Atlanta to get to New York. In Atlanta I deplaned just to walk around for a few minutes. It was nearly midnight by that time and occasionally Santa Claus was paged over the public address system. I found no humor or joy in that Christmas; in fact, bitterness was setting in.

I still could not understand why my parents had to be my enemies. They never knew the Church as I had known it, mostly because I had not been allowed to share it with them. They felt in competition with the Church and I could understand why. Was it my inability to understand God's will for my life, or was I making a mistake?

We arrived at LaGuardia airport at 5:00 A.M. Christmas morning. I did not have enough money to catch a cab into the city, so I would have to wait for the buses to start running. That gave me two hours to sit and think.

I think it was symbolic that I sat in that gigantic, deserted terminal. My life felt vacant and empty. My doubts about Moon swirled through my head as I sat there. I realized that I had given up my parents, my education, my money, my car, my job—everything that I possessed—for something that I was not sure of.

In a prayer that morning as I sat in the empty airport, I told God that I was willing to give up everything for him and that I would not resent what had happened if I could just be sure of his will for my life. I was scared, lonely, and tired.

When I got back to the Center that morning I expected to find a festive atmosphere. But there were only a few odd decorations up in the house, and everyone that was up seemed to be depressed. It was obvious that they all missed their families.

Tom was less than cordial. I couldn't wait to tell him the harrowing story of my last forty-eight hours. When he saw me, he said dryly, "Where have you been?" No embrace, no handshake, no "Merry Christmas," just judgment. "I told you to be back before Christmas."

"Tom," I said, "I have nearly been deprogrammed. The reason you have not been able to reach me is that my parents changed their phone number so no one could call me."

"Why didn't you call us?" he asked.

"I don't know. With you being over 2000 miles away somehow I didn't think there was anything you could do to help my situation."

"I have assigned Pat to be the editor of the paper. You are going to be sent to Barrytown for training," he said unemotionally.

"Why?" I pleaded. "I have done my best."

"You need training. You don't know the Principle well enough."

I had known it well enough to be teaching it. His drastic change of attitude about me was devastating. At Barrytown I would be subjected to no less than twelve hours of lectures a day for at least forty days and maybe as long as 120. Most left Barrytown changed people—and changed in a way I did not want to be.

Tom assigned another brother to stay with me at all times, using the excuse that a deprogrammer might try to grab me off the street if I was alone. I knew that he was putting a constant watch on me in order that I might not just up and leave.

It was finally coming to this: I was being forced to sell out the last thing that I had left—me! If I went to Barrytown I would come away from there a changed person. Not necessarily brainwashed, but totally dependent. I would be like a child, willing to let others make my decisions and would have a childlike, unquestioning loyalty. I wouldn't necessarily get my doubts about the Church resolved as much as I would finally bury my doubts under layers of indoctrination. Children are controlled because they are dependent. The same applies to a member of the Unification Church.

We spent several of the next few days at Moon's estate in Tarry-town celebrating one of Moon's holidays, God's Day. Most of the east coast movement was there and I was able to visit and reminisce with friends.

I saw Marc Lee at the festivities, and we slipped off to a Howard Johnson's to have a cup of coffee and talk.

"You've been to Barrytown?" I asked in amazement.

"Yeah," he said. "I really fought going for a long time. I felt like I didn't need it. But it has really changed me. I have much more peace now."

I watched him as he talked, and I could indeed see that he was much more peaceful. Yet, I was uncomfortable with his willingness to do "anything that Father asked." Before, Marc had tempered his loyalty with common sense.

"Anything, Marc?" I asked disappointedly.

"Anything!" Marc replied.

I wasn't sure if he was just trying to impress me or if he really meant it. And I was afraid to know. Realizing though, that Barrytown seemed to be the source of the change even further convinced me that I did not want to go. While talking with Marc, I suddenly realized that I was going to have to leave the Unification Church in order to discover if it was real or not.

Ever since I had escaped from Carlsbad I had not been able to sleep at night. I could almost hear voices inside my head arguing over what I should do. Most nights I lay awake all night long.

On the morning of January 5, 1976, I woke up with a clear thought in my mind: "Get up and leave."

"But, where can I go?" I asked myself.

"Get up and leave." I heard it again.

Trusting that voice, I got up. It was not even five yet, and no one else was awake. The suitcases that I had brought from Carlsbad still remained packed, so leaving would be easy. I would have to tiptoe over several bodies sleeping on the floor, but most Family members slept so soundly that they were difficult to awaken.

It was cold when I stepped out to the corner of 107th and Broadway. I didn't know where I was going. I just wanted to get away. At that moment, I felt the farther the better.

I remember thinking that this action determined my fate one way or the other. If Moon really was the Christ, I was betraying him and was no better than a Judas. If I was right and Moon really wasn't the messiah, then I was like a prodigal son returning home after squandering all my riches. One way or the other. There was no fence sitting; it was either black or white, right or wrong.

I walked up to a pay phone and dialed a long distance number collect. I heard the operator say, "A collect call for anyone from Chris Elkins. Will you accept the charges?"

I heard a sleepy voice say, "Yes, operator."

The operator said, "Go ahead."

"Travis?"

"Yeah," he said, "where are you?"

"New York. I guess you made it away from Carlsbad all right."

"More or less. But, how are you?"

"I need some place to go, Travis. I am leaving the Unification Church."

"You're not going to go home?" he asked.

"No," I said, "I'm afraid that Mom and Dad will still try the deprogramming. I need to work this thing out on my own—it's between me and God."

"Well then," he said, "you're gonna come here, aren't you?"

"If it's all right with you."

Laughing, Travis said, "I have a crowded apartment, no money, and don't have all the answers myself, but whatever I have, just consider it yours."

"I'll catch a plane down there and call you when I arrive," I replied.

"I'll be looking for you. And, we're going to work this thing out, Chris."

"Thank you, Travis."

When I turned away from that phone the world was a brighter place. I had hope, confidence, and someone who loved me in spite of my mistakes.

16

The House Subcommittee on International Organizations
September 27, 1976
Washington, D.C.

I wish I could say that I woke up the next day after arriving at Travis's with the whole thing figured out. But, I didn't. It was all boiling down to the issue of whether Moon was the messiah or not. My two and a half years of pain and sacrifice were justifiable if he really was Christ, but all was in folly if he wasn't.

I can't even tell you of a particular day that I finally came to the conclusion that Moon was not the Christ. It wasn't within the first week, and probably not within the first month. I paced the floor a lot, I searched, and I prayed.

Going to Travis was one of the best things that happened. With him I felt no pressure to work it all out in a set period of time. He couldn't necessarily help me with my spiritual problems, but he provided for me a security that I needed in order for the Holy Spirit to open my eyes.

I didn't go back to church the next Sunday, either. I feared the reaction of Christians to an ex-Moonie more than I feared the reaction of any other group of people. The last thing I needed at the time was more rejection.

It was a month before I could contact Mom and Dad, too. In my initial contact I wrote them, "I know that you have been deeply hurt. I don't expect you to forget the hurt, but try to forgive me. No one

135

aches any more over what has happened than I."

Initially they were apprehensive. They weren't sure whether I had really left the Church or not. I know that they wanted to believe it, but did not want to get hurt again. Our relationship healed, and as with a broken arm, it has mended back stronger than before.

I had a debt to settle with God, too. He had been patient with me. I really believe that I had a genuine conversion experience at the age of ten. The tragedy that occurred in my life was not due to a lack of salvation, but out of a lack of Christian maturity. In fact, had Jesus not come into my life when I was ten I don't know how I would have ever been able to come out of the movement.

Yes, I denied Christ while I was a member of that movement. But, Peter denied Christ three times, and there is not a Christian alive now that has not somehow denied Christ in thought, word, or deed. My Savior accepted me "just as I am"—faults and all. He didn't condone my actions, but I don't think that he ever stopped loving me.

Although Travis never pressured me about money, I did, within two weeks, go to work. And not only at one job, but two. Keeping busy was important at first.

The day job I had was at a finance company. Oddly enough, they hired me on the spot and did not check my two and a half years with the Freedom Leadership Foundation. I told them that it was a political organization. They were more concerned with my past financial experience.

A lady that worked with me at the finance company did more to get me back on the right track than did anyone else. Although she was the busiest person in the office she always found time to pay special attention to me. She had no idea I had ever been a Moonie. No one did. But often she would bring me a piece of pie she had baked, or share part of her lunch with me. Her smile was a blessing, and she took the time to care. She was a healing ointment in my life, and she never realized it. She showed me that there were really Christians that did care. And that there were those secure enough in their beliefs to share them. I needed that.

I read as much as I could find about the Second Coming of Christ. The Scriptures warned so clearly in several places of those who would come bearing a striking resemblance to the real thing. They might even fool the very elect among us. When I read of those warnings it came alive to me. It reminded me of the nuns, seminarians, doctors, and lawyers that I knew who were followers of Moon.

Everything I could discover about Jesus kept leading me to the conclusion that Moon was not the Christ. He did not follow the pattern or ways of the prophets that God had sent before. Nor did his advent even closely resemble the advent of Christ that God has promised.

More than anything else, I had to do something with the Moonies' view of the fall of man. It was shown to me by several people that it was not important *what* the fruit of the tree of knowledge of good and evil really was. It was not the *fruit* that caused the fall. It was *Eve's desire to be like God,* and have her eyes opened like his. It was that desire which caused Eve to fall, not the lure of a delicious fruit or a sexual relationship.

And, in my estimation, Moon is offering his members the same thing that caused Eve to fall—perfection. They believe that someday they and their progeny will be rid of sin through a process of working off the sin debt accumulated by one's ancestry. The Church calls this "indemnity." This desire to be perfect led mankind away from God in the first place, and I believe the same thing is happening among the members of the Unification Church.

Fear was the last thing I conquered.

There was that silence that day in the caucus room. And again I wished that Greg, the research assistant, hadn't asked the reporters to leave. Their questions I could handle; the stares of anger and hatred from my ex-Moonie friends behind me I couldn't handle. I heard my name being whispered. And as I turned slightly, I saw several looking at me. Out of the corner of my eye I detected heads shaking. Some started moving down to seats closer to mine.

And had my watch stopped? Two-thirty. It seemed that it was two-thirty ten minutes ago. A hush settled into the room.

Fear. I feared what they might say about me, or how they might damage my character by slandering me. Suddenly, I realized that although I no longer took orders from them or even lived with them, that they still manipulated me—through fear. How, possibly, could I overcome that?

I knew what I'd have to do; but would I have the strength? As I stood up, the whispering stopped. Turning to face them was probably the hardest thing I have ever had to do in my whole life. As

I walked back, my legs shook and my whole body trembled.

God, give me the strength! I prayed silently.

I extended my hand to one of them. I spoke; my voice trembled. I don't even remember what I said. I shook hands with others, and still others. The love of God would triumph!

They, in turn, grew quiet, not understanding the source of my strength. A few minutes later I was able to talk and express my love for them.

It was proven to me how much stronger love is than hate. They could have out-hated me easily, but they could never have out-loved me. I loved them in spite of their mistakes, the same way that God was loving me. They loved me when I did what they wanted me to do, but once I broke ranks, their love dispersed. That kind of love is cheap.

A bank teller is trained to spot a counterfeit bill in one way. He's trained to know the real thing so well that a counterfeit will never fool him.

There's a lesson in that about love. God's love is the real thing. Once you have known it, everything else seems fake.

CONCLUSION

Rarely does a day go by that I don't talk to anguished parents whose children have become Moonies. Their desperation and agony are heartbreaking. Their confusion is considerable, and a million questions haunt them: "What did we do wrong?" "Wasn't our love good enough?" "Should we have been more strict?" "Why do our children hate us now?" "Has my child been brainwashed?" and "Should we hire a deprogrammer?"

The church is involved in this too, or at least ought to be. It's easy, in the aftermath of the Jim Jones People's Temple tragedy, for Christians' grief to become mingled with a certain smugness: "After all, if only they had been Christians none of this would have happened." But, of course, that's not the appropriate response— many of them *are* Christians, or at least came from Christian churches, *our* churches and Sunday schools. In fact, you'll find that many in the Unification Church have been drawn away from mainstream denominations; lots of them are Jewish or Catholic— or Evangelical.

Now I don't have all the answers. These are difficult problems, and I don't mean to convey the impression that mothers and fathers and pastors and Sunday school teachers are all wrong, that they have completely failed. As it was in my case, the fault lay at the feet of many   myself included. But the Unification Church, as evil as it may be, is only taking advantage of situations that Christians have helped create. And perhaps through my experience others can learn something about the processes of thought and feeling that a young person goes through when he or she is touched by a cult.

Parents should be comforted by the fact that 50 percent of all Moonies eventually leave the Unification Church, many of them walking away out of their own free will. The Moonies' harmony and blissful love is something that rarely lasts. Disillusionment is common in the Unification Church.

Furthermore, I don't believe that Moonies are brainwashed. There is certainly a good deal of indoctrination, lots of teaching, and even a reorientation of values and authority, but I have never seen evidence of blatant chemical or mechanical brainwashing.

This makes everything more difficult. If brainwashing does not take place (and at least there is considerable doubt that it does), then deprogramming—the process of forcefully reorienting a person back to his or her original convictions—is a dangerous thing to do. Parents don't understand that the Unification Church has taught their children to doubt them as parents, to mistrust their love, and to consider them motivated by Satan. When a parent sends a deprogrammer out after his child, all of these teachings are confirmed in the young person's mind. From a Moonie's perspective, then, what evidence is there of a parent's love?

Parents, don't consider deprogramming as a solution to your problem. Statistics show that many Moonies who have been deprogrammed eventually return to the Unification Church with more conviction and resolve than ever before. And in some cases, deprogramming does serious damage to the mind. There *is* hope for a Moonie through conventional means of prayer and abundant love; but those who are deprogrammed have a greater chance of being lost forever.

The Unification Church wins its members through love and doctrine. So often the reason a young person becomes a Moonie is so he or she can be more closely linked with God. As well, these people want to be associated with others who love the Lord and have a vision of hope. And it's ironic that they leave our churches to find these things.

I was intrigued by three things in Moon's Church: authority, love, and mission. I did not believe in the doctrine of Moon so much because it was sensible and true, but because I had faith in the leaders and teachers who presented it to me. To me, the assurance of being told what was true was more attractive than the uncertainty and difficulty of finding out the truth for myself. "Aha!" those of us in the Christian church say, "this is it; authority is the key. Christians should place their authority in the Bible, not in men." And, of course, this is true—Christians *should* put their faith in the Bible, not in men. But doesn't the Christian Church go against its own advice? Don't Christians elevate certain people to a celebrity status, and then place their trust in them? In fact, Christianity is loaded with so many experts and great teachers and Christian leaders that to some unsuspecting souls the Rev. Moon is just another star in the galaxy.

Perhaps the hardest thing to refute in the Unification Church is the love that its members share. The lure of such intimate and unselfish communion is a strong influence on someone who feels alone and afraid in the world. And many young people, especially, feel alone and afraid. No wonder the Unification Church is successful!

Now I believe that this love is a genuine love, but not a Christian love. And there lies an answer. *The love of Christ that Christians share ought to be greater than the love that Moonies share together*.

But so often it isn't. In fact, in my experience, one of the primary reasons I joined the Unification Church was because of the rejection and distrust that I felt at the hands of Christian people. Christians, be warm and loving and caring to Moonies you may meet in your lives: genuine Christian love is something that a Moonie just can't handle—it challenges everything he has been taught.

Finally, I was lured into the Unification Church by people who *acted* upon what they believed. After years of being a Christian whose beliefs didn't *mean* anything in terms of commitment or sacrifice, I was exhilarated to give all of myself to Moon. It was, at least for a time, something that gave my life some significance.

Now I don't want to say that all churches lack this kind of commitment and sacrifice in their Christianity. But some certainly do, and it's a weakness that Moon exploits all too well. He knows (as perhaps we do not) that young people have the time, energy, and will to give—it's just a question of who's going to take it. So far, Moon has a monopoly on it.

Ultimately, everything funnels down to what is *true*. Just as I finally addressed all of my doubts with the question, "Is Moon the messiah?" so that is the question that plagues the Unification Church. It is the truth of Christ that we must proclaim. And not just the facts of his life and about the Bible, but the *truth* one experiences when one engages in the mystery of Christ. When it came down to it for me, the truth of Jesus Christ clearly outshone the ploys and tactics of Moon.

Indeed, this is our hope as ex-Moonies and frightened parents and bewildered pastors and Sunday school teachers, as expressed in John 8:32: "Ye shall know the truth, and the truth shall make you free."